PARENTS, TAKE CHARGE!

Parents, Take Charge!

Perry L. Draper

LIVING STUDIES
Tyndale House Publishers, Inc.
Wheaton, Illinois

Acknowledgments

Material reprinted by permission from *The Christian
Family,* by Larry Christenson, published and copyright
1970, Bethany Fellowship, Inc., Minneapolis,
Minnesota 55438.

Material from *An Answer to Parent-Teen
Relationships,* by Norman Wright, copyright 1977,
Harvest House Publishers, 1075 Arrowsmith, Eugene,
Oregon 97402, used by permission.

Quoted material adapted from "How to Understand the
Perplexing Teenager" by Roy W. Menninger M.D.,
Reader's Digest, March 1972, used by permission.

Permission to reproduce the chart from *Help! I'm a
Parent!* by Bruce Narramore, copyright © 1972,
Zondervan Publishing House. Used by permission.

The chart from chapter 2 of *Child Behavior* by Frances
L. Ilg, M.D. and Louise Bates Ames, Ph.D. Copyright
1955 by Frances L. Ilg and Louise Bates Ames.
Reprinted by permission of Harper & Row, Publishers,
Inc.

Material reprinted by permission of the author and
publisher in Virginia Satir's *Conjoint Family Therapy,*
Science & Behavior Books, Inc., Palo Alto, California,
1967.

Material from *Raising a Hyperactive Child,* by Mark A.
Stewart, M.D., and Sally Wendkos Olds. Copyright ©
1973 by Mark A. Stewart. Reprinted by permission of
Harper & Row, Publishers, Inc. (pp. 36, 37).

All Scripture references are taken from the *New
International Version* (NIV) of the Bible, unless
otherwise noted.

First printing, July 1982
Library of Congress Catalog Card Number 81-86695
ISBN 0-8423-4822-0
Copyright © 1982 by Perry L. Draper
All rights reserved
Printed in the United States of America

Contents

One

The Task

Remember the day you brought your first little one home from the hospital? You felt like you owned the world as you held that little bundle of joy complete with dimples. You couldn't get your eyes off him or her. Many of your hopes and dreams welled up from deep within your soul. A pleasant warm feeling grew inside. "Look what we produced!" Everything was wonderful and the world was beautiful.

Two weeks later, haggard, baggy-eyed, weary, you were pacing the floor with a screaming child, wondering to yourself, "Where did I go wrong? It wasn't supposed to be like this! I changed her, fed her, burped her, but nothing worked. The book doesn't tell me any more to do. What do I do now? Maybe I'm not cut out to be a parent!" You were stuck at obstacle number one. But this was only the beginning of many hurdles yet to be overcome.

Goals

Few of us would start out on a journey without an idea of where we are going, what we are going to do when we get there, and the basic steps along the way to reach our destination. But not many parents have taken the time and careful thought to determine what sort of child they wish to bring up, the basic goals they have for this child, and the various steps toward reaching those goals. The following statements give a few clues as to differing parental goals:

"Children should be seen and not heard."
"Children are like buds that just need a bit of en-
couragement in order to blossom."
"I don't want my kids to have to struggle as I did."
"I want my kids to be obedient at all times. When I
speak, I expect action, now!"
"Kids are fine as long as they don't interfere with
what I want to do."
"I want my kids to be the best in everything."
"I want my kids to stand up and fight so that no-
body can walk all over them."
"I just want my kids to be happy."
"I just want my kids to grow up in a normal home
and find their best potential."

Each statement suggests definite goals that greatly
influence the manner in which we raise our children, and
what we consider success or failure basically to be. Our desired goals will govern our attitudes toward our children—
whether we consider them "good" kids or "bad" kids, a
disappointment or a joy to us. Our outlook will govern our
treatment of them on a day-to-day basis, and will also affect
our long-range choices.

Parental Training

Where did you get your training as a parent? What
parent-training school or college did you attend or graduate
from? Have you taken any courses in marriage and family?

Our major training usually has come from our
own *parental and home background.* As a small child we
observed and listened. We noted everything that our parents
said and did, their basic attitudes, the way they solved problems, how they talked to other people, and their own basic
direction in life. It is no accident that the tough kid in frequent fights on the block comes from a home where one
parent or the other is also a scrappy individual, or has a
"tough-guy" attitude. Generally speaking, kids who grow up
to be sociable and caring and interested in others come from
homes where the parents were caring, sociable, and reached
out to others in need. Kids who tend to be shy and fearful
often have had one or both parents who were shy and fearful.

The example of parents deeply influences the child.

At times, you will find a child who seems to go to the opposite extreme, somewhat out of rebellion and disgust with the parents' values. Such is a child who becomes very rebellious, getting into frequent trouble as a reaction to the overstrictness and straitlaced patterns of his parents. Likewise, a child of very irresponsible parents (for instance, in a home with a lot of drinking and fighting) may grow up to be a very conscientious, peace-loving child. Such a child is reacting against his parents' values, an example which he finds disgusting. These are more the exception than the rule.

Taking a Long-Range View

Child raising is basically a *twenty-year project.*[1] Even if that perfect little angel has become the perfect devil within the space of only a few hours, all is not lost! A good dose of patience, persistence, and firmness will get him turned in the right direction again.

Most parents will want their child to be prepared to take on the responsibilities of life, able to support himself, get married, raise a family of his own, find a career, and advance himself, all without undue dependence upon his parents. What a tremendous contrast to the tiny babe that was brought home from the hospital, unable to feed himself, change himself, move around in any fashion, or do much of anything for himself! The following two diagrams, showing the changing process of parental control and child responsibility, give an idea of the overall task.

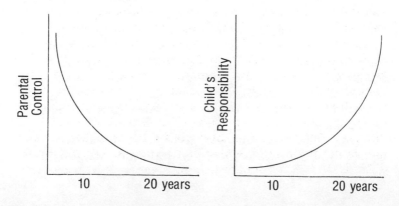

The tiny babe is totally unprepared to take the responsibilities that the world requires. He needs his parents' protection, attention, time, and training. By the same token, an eighteen-year-old would be totally incensed, angry, and frustrated by a parent who would seek to exercise the amount of control more appropriate for a five-year-old child. The gradual step-by-step process of less and less parental control, shifting to more and more responsibility on the part of the child, prepares the child by somewhere around eighteen to twenty to complete his transition and be on his own without undue trauma.

By contrast, a pathological home with troubled parents will usually do one of two things. 1) The parents will attempt to keep too tight a control and protection for much too long, never teaching the child to think for himself or learn to face responsibility; 2) the parent may have very inadequate controls, thus allowing the child to be exposed to many things he is quite unprepared to handle; then rebellion and irresponsibility follow. As a result, the child has not been taught to face the responsibilities of life, is unprepared for adulthood, and is frankly scared and insecure with the forbidding world before him. Note that either extreme may produce the same results.

Overly tight control

> anxiety, insecurity, immaturity

Very inadequate control

Parents as Chief Trainers

Proverbs 22:6 tells us, "Train up a child in the way he should go, and when he is old he will not depart from it." The parent is depicted as a *trainer.*

From this passage, the strong implications of two ingredients come through: 1) a definite way to train a child; and 2) the fact that if properly done, the child's later maturing process will demonstrate the years of effort and input of the parent in a productive life style, one that the parent can be reasonably proud of.

The Scriptures do give definite standards and values to be taught, learned, and followed. Many of these basics are similar to the legal code of our land, and thus are essential to peace and a relatively hassle-free life in our communities. In addition, there are many choices between the "acceptable, the good, the better, and the best" of life that make the difference between a humdrum existence and a productive, happy life.

There is also the strong implication that "the way he should go . . ." (from the verse in Proverbs) may not be exactly the same for every child. Certain basics will remain the same, of course. It will be wrong to steal, to kill, to lie — for any child. But the way these values are taught and applied may vary somewhat, depending on the individual child. Thus, some have translated this passage, "Train up a child according to his way," implying respect for the individuality of the child.[2]

Anyone with several children recognizes well that each one is a separate personality, distinct and different from others in the family, and responds differently to the same circumstances. Some are quite timid, and need a lot of loving encouragement. Some are boisterous and irresponsible and need a lot of firm discipline and structure to keep them on the track. Still others are already quite conscientious and self-disciplined and need help in developing creativity and freedom of self-expression. The basics of right and wrong remain the same for each, but the application to each personality is different.

A football coach takes a green recruit and teaches him some basics in a relatively sheltered atmosphere, gradually exposing him to more and more of the rough and tumble, with continual practice, until finally he is able to enter the game. Even then, the coach will continue to stretch him further by encouragement, instruction, and correction, with increasing exposure to the tougher parts of the game, until he is able to handle himself well. The coach has thus produced a good player who can stand the hard knocks and think his way through new and different situations.

The main responsibility for training the children in the way they should go is not placed upon the schools, nor the community, nor the churches, as important as each of these may be. The one institution that has by far the most time with and influence upon the child is the *family,* and more specifically the *parents.* Each of the others *may* have good influence. The school provides academic discipline which is vital to an effective, productive life. The community provides a consciousness and sensitivity to the human need, likewise valuable to balance in life. The church provides the spiritual dimension to life, a set of values, a consciousness of right and wrong, and a personal faith in a living God, made available through Christ the Son of God. Each of these is vital to a happy, productive, and useful life. But none of these has the same opportunity as parents in the direct planting of attitudes, values, philosophy of life, habits, temperaments, sense of responsibility, dependability, etc. Children watch what their parents do and copy their actions. Children hear what their parents say and tend to follow their ways of saying things. Children even sense what parents feel and absorb many of these feelings as their own.

Because of their dependency on their parents for the basic necessities of life itself, small children do not compare their parents with others, as they are in no position to do so. No one else is that important to them. Only when they become teenagers and reach out to other friends do they begin to compare, to any great degree, how other parents behave. By that time, however, many of the patterns are deeply set within and come out in later adulthood as behavior of the individual himself. It is, therefore, not an accident that a child who grows up in a home that is full of physical violence and abuse will tend to become in later life an abusive parent or spouse himself. The values which he has learned from his own parents become his own values, which he easily carries on. Thus, both positive and negative traits can be carried on for generations, passed on from parent to child without even thinking about it.

The journey through child raising must start in the beginning with you as a parent. What kind of children will you bring up? They'll probably be very much like yourself. Honestly, do you want your children to be like you? Are you happy with yourself as an individual? It would be well at this point to take time to answer the question, "What kind of person am I?" The following is a listing of sample personal characteristics. Ask yourself, "Where do I fit in with each of these?"

impatient	vs.	patient
hot-tempered	vs.	cool, even-tempered
cold and distant	vs.	warm and affectionate
opinionated	vs.	considerate of others' ideas
prejudiced	vs.	accepting
jealous	vs.	content
self-righteous	vs.	humble
argumentative	vs.	peaceful
impulsive and unpredictable	vs.	self-controlled
stingy	vs.	generous
rude	vs.	courteous
sneaky and secretive	vs.	open and honest
phony	vs.	sincere
rigid and narrow-minded	vs.	broad-minded
demanding	vs.	tolerant
passive	vs.	assertive
dependent	vs.	self-confident
disorganized	vs.	methodical
impulsive	vs.	self-disciplined
anxious and worrisome	vs.	relaxed
pessimistic	vs.	cheerful and optimistic
nonaffectionate	vs.	affectionate
critical	vs.	accepting
punitive	vs.	forgiving
self-absorbed	vs.	sensitivity to others' needs
partial	vs.	fair-minded
emotionally inhibited	vs.	spontaneous and uninhibited
irresponsible	vs.	dependable and reasonable

Note the areas where you are strong and thank God for those strengths. They will probably show up in your children.

Note the areas where you are weak. Go to work on each of these.

Didn't do too well? Don't despair. You don't have to be locked into negative traits for the rest of your life. Nor do you have to be a perfect parent before you can launch your kids in this life. They wouldn't fit in too well if they were perfect anyway. Angels are hard to relate to on earth. The characteristics listed are simply goals to work toward, and growth toward these goals is a *process*, with gradual change taking place on a day-to-day basis over the months and years. The point is that a parent who is growing and learning will produce children who are growing and learning.

Remember that you are not alone in the growing process. God is very interested in your personal growth, and will see to it that different experiences come your way to help you grow. Philippians 1:6 tells us, "He who began a good work in you, will carry it on to completion until the day of Jesus Christ." The picture is of a process of growth working toward the definite goal of becoming Christlike. But the process will not become complete until the day we meet Christ face to face.

There are definite things we must do in order to help that process along. The Apostle Paul said in Philippians 3:12, 13:

> Not that I have already obtained all this, or have already been made perfect, but I press on to take hold of that for which Christ Jesus took hold of me. . . . But this one thing I do: Forgetting what is behind and straining toward what is ahead, I press on toward the goal to win the prize for which God has called me heavenward in Christ Jesus.

Here again is a process: 1) putting aside false pride which says I am already perfect, 2) forgiving self for being human, and letting go of the past, 3) making conscious effort to grow, to press on, 4) a final goal of becoming Christlike in behavior and the inner person, something I work toward but have by no means yet reached.

The task of reaching forward to the goal of Christlike behavior is not something that suddenly jumps out at us, or mysteriously descends upon us by a special miracle of God. It comes in a day-to-day commitment to God for the purpose of growth according to his divine plan.

The Apostle Paul explained in Romans 12:1, 2:

> Therefore, I urge you, brothers, in view of God's mercy, to offer your bodies as living sacrifices, holy and pleasing to God—which is your spiritual worship. Do not conform any longer to the pattern of this world, but be transformed by the renewing of your mind. Then you will be able to test and approve what God's will is—his good, pleasing and perfect will.

The answer to this daily growth process is found by: 1) a daily commitment to God—giving him all of your inner desires, attitudes, and inner self and 2) a renewed thinking pattern that seeks to think God's thoughts, not those of the world system and its self-centered philosophy. The point is simply to commit yourself to God each day, consciously holding nothing back; to consciously put away the self-centered, get-even, grasping ways of this world; think on the ways of God, the attitudes of acceptance, compassion, forgiveness, and desire for straight living found in the model of Christ, who reveals the characteristics of the Father to us. The result will be a demonstration of the will of God, or to say it another way, our lives will demonstrate the desirable Christlike behavior.

As you grow in this way, you will be pleased with the outcome both in your children's lives and in your own.

Workbook Section Chapter One

1. *Thinking through.*
Take ten minutes to think. What type of child would you like to have? List as many specific characteristics as you can think of: e.g., aggressive, a fighter, quiet, instantly obedient, all "A" student, hard worker, creative, playful, etc.

7) gentle	12) intelligent
8) hard worker	2) open & honest
6) creative	3) affectionate ✓
9) playful ✓	11) accepting
5) assertive	4) dependable
10) thoughtful	13) generous
1) concerned about others ✓	

Think again. Are any of these unrealistic? Are any insignificant? If so, cross them out.

Now go back and try to put some priority numbers on those you think are the most important to develop, e.g., 1, 2, 3, etc.

Now, how are you doing on those important ones? Grade yourself on your progress with each: E-excellent, G-good, I-improvement needed. Take the age of the child into account in your evaluation.

Which ones need special attention right now? Put a check beside these.

2. *Control and responsibility.*
Draw in the following graphs your *own* progress in letting go of control over the years and for turning over responsibility to your child.

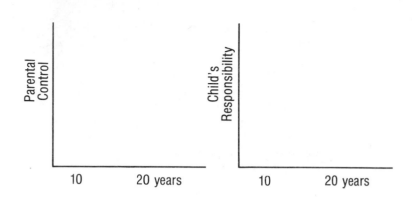

Is some of this moving too fast? Is some of it moving too slowly? Draw in a dotted line how you would like it to progress.

3. *Your personal growth.*

Go back over the listing of personal characteristics in the text from page 13. List below the ones in which you are the strongest:

[handwritten: open + honest]

[handwritten: broad minded]

[handwritten: forgiving]

[handwritten: dependable ✓]

[handwritten: + reasonable]

[handwritten: sincere]

[handwritten: methodical]

Build on these. Make a conscious daily effort to develop each of these further, to become even more skillful and effective than you are now. Check the ones you are strongest in. List afterward the areas where you are not so strong.

[handwritten: impatient ✓]   *[handwritten: self righteous]*

[handwritten: impulsive]   *[handwritten: punitive ✓]*

[handwritten: passive]

Which of these is your worst? Put a check beside it. Focus on this one for the next month. Ask God for his daily help in overcoming this problem.

Copy both the positive and negative characteristics on another piece of paper for quick reference, or use this sheet. Refer to it daily. Commit your life each day to God to work toward the goals of: 1) improving your positive characteristics, and 2) improving your areas of weakness.

Review your progress from month to month and roughly graph your progress over the next year.

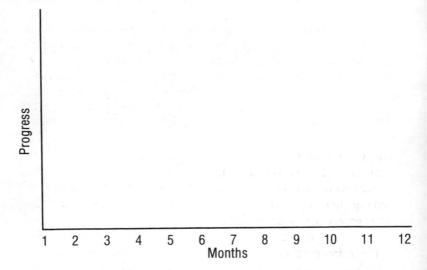

[1]Henry R. Brandt and Homer E. Dowdy, *Building a Christian Home* (Wheaton, Ill.: Scripture Press, 1960), p. 104.

[2]Derek Kidner, *The Proverbs, The Tyndale Old Testament Commentaries*, ed. D. J. Wiseman (Downers Grove, Ill.: InterVarsity Press, 1976), p. 147.

Two

The Family as a Unit

The parents of a small child have laid careful plans to go out for the evening while someone baby-sits during the child's normal sleeping time. The moment they are to step out the door, the child abruptly awakes and begins to cry, becomes cranky, and refuses to be comforted. This happens on repeated occasions. It would appear that the child somehow knows when the parents are going out.

A stubborn, strong-willed child instinctively knows where his father and mother are unsure of their ground and may differ with each other. He exploits this weakness by bringing the parents to a place of self-doubt or setting them in conflict with one another, in order to get his own way. Confusion follows.

A child grows up in a family which finds difficulty in facing problems squarely and working them out to a satisfactory conclusion. Without continued parental help, the child remains dependent, immature, and unable to face his own problems in growing up.

A child grows up in a home where parents shy away from any sort of conflict. This child grows up being easily intimidated and harassed by other kids, and quite unable to defend himself adequately.

A father and son are locked into bitter clashes with each other while the mother stands helplessly by, worried that someone will be hurt, or the family will be permanently fractured in some way. The conflict never gets settled but goes on and on for years.

A runaway daughter, frequently in trouble, has

been considered the "black sheep" of the family, a "problem child." From the beginning the parents never expected her to amount to much.

A child who is chronically a problem, a source of grief and heartache to the family, finally leaves home permanently. Instead of the family now drawing closer together, out of relief from the conflict, the family falls apart and the father and mother separate.

What is going on? How can these happenings be explained?

All of the above are illustrations of different aspects in which the family acts as a unit, or system, in which each member is inseparably related to the other, but all functioning as a whole. There are no isolated parents or isolated individuals within the family, anymore than the hand or the foot is a completely separate, isolated part of the body. Each is related to the other and interdependent on the other as a member of one complete unit.

Similar teaching is presented in 1 Corinthians 12: 24-27 concerning the inter-relationship of one fellow believer with another. Every believer is a child of God by the new birth, and thus a member of God's family, and a part of a large body of believers (v. 27). But no one is a separate individual himself, to be and do what he alone wants, without affecting the others who are also fellow believers and part of the body of Christ. Each one is important in his own right, yet, each is quite intertwined with others.

Parents at the Center of the Family

The primary relationship within the family is that of the father and the mother. What the parents do as a team together directly affects the development, growth, self-worth, and future of each family member. More specifically, how parents relate to each other as husband and wife directly affects the development of each child's personality, his relationship to others, male-female relationships, and the kind of family that each child will, himself or herself, set up in later life.

Clinical practice has demonstrated a basic rule in family development which may be stated as follows: *A*

healthy relationship between the husband and wife tends to
produce good parenting and secure children who are in turn
able to produce normal family relationships. A pained marital relationship tends to produce defective parenting, which
in turn tends to produce troubled children.[1]

Illustration #1

Illustration #1 indicates a picture of a healthy
family relationship in which the husband and wife have a
strong bond together, are emotionally close, treat each other
as number one in their lives, and together love their children. This in turn provides an atmosphere conducive to security and personal growth within the children.

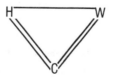

Illustration #2

Illustration #2 indicates a picture of a problem
family. In this case, the husband and wife are united by their
children. This may show up in an overly positive or overly
negative way. In the positive way, the parents may lavish
affection and material goods on the child, trying to show
their love by giving the child what he or she wants, implying
that the child is of supreme worth and nothing is too good
for him. However, instead of seeing positive results, they
produce a spoiled, self-centered child who is ill prepared to
cope with adult life. From the negative point of view, the
child may become the receiver of many put-downs and criti-

cisms, or may become a source of constant irritation to the
parents and be a sore spot to them. The child may become
the "black sheep" who is always out of step with the rest of
the family, or the "scapegoat" to receive the brunt of others'
hostility, blame, and frustration that the family members actually feel for each other. The parents are thus dumping their
problems on the child.

      Regardless of which way it is presented, the child
gets the attention of both parents, which in turn provides the
family's main bond, thus providing the basic glue for the
marriage to stick together. As long as the child is the focus of
attention, either in a positive adoring way, or in a negative
degrading way, the marriage holds together. It becomes the
basic responsibility of the child to remain either the "angel"
or the "devil" of the family so as to keep the marriage together to unite the family, a tremendous responsibility for
any child. The child may do this by developing a number of
behavioral problems which require the frequent attention of
husband and wife, and thus keep some kind of relationship
going. The "bad" child attempts to hold the family together
with the firm belief that a sick family is better than no family.

      Any experienced counselor has learned of cases in
which the kids are valiantly trying to get their father and
mother back together long after the marriage has died, and
severely blame themselves for not being successful.

      Any changes in this kind of system pose a threat
to the already precarious security of the husband and wife.
Thus, there is resistance to growth or a healthier life style.

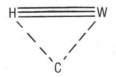

Illustration #3

      Illustration #3 indicates another kind of problem
family. On the surface, it appears that there is a very strong

bond between husband and wife. However, neither parent has adequately matured; both are overly dependent upon each other and are too wrapped up in their own personal needs to have enough time for or interest in their children. The parents become overly involved with each other, losing their own individuality in the relationship. The parents themselves never quite grew up, and thus the child remains immature, self-centered, unloved, and unable to become an autonomous person.

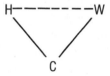

Illustration #4

Illustration #4 indicates the family disintegration. The child grows up, leaves home, or in some way leaves the inner circle of the family. At this point an unhealthy marriage bond of husband and wife is severely threatened. The parents may begin blaming each other for being too harsh, or for spoiling the child, whichever the case may be. The parents then become locked into conflict with each other. As the unhealthy relationship continues to degenerate, any one of the following may happen: 1) the husband and wife triangulate to include a third person in an extramarital affair; 2) the husband and wife may decide to separate and divorce; or 3) they may remain together but essentially as two separate people under the same roof, living in an emotional desert.

Clinical experience indicates a second basic rule of family development: *As a husband and wife begin to work on their own personal problems and grow closer emotionally, become more interested in each other, and are of greater importance to each other, behavior problems of their children begin to improve.* At this point, the children tend to respond to most of the management techniques that parents may use, whether they be spankings, restrictions, positive reinforcements, etc.

Clinical observations also indicate that when husband and wife are not close emotionally, and are more involved in their children than they are in each other, the children's behavior tends to regress and grow worse. At this point, any management approaches of the parents tend to become unsuccessful and the child becomes unmanageable. The symptoms of an inner family relationship weakness emerges.[2]

Parents as the Child's First Teacher

As indicated in Chapter One, the very small child observes carefully everything his parents do and the ways he does them. Since he has no other real comparison, he takes what he sees as "this is the way it is done," and generally follows the same way (there are some exceptions to every rule). Thus, for a full five years the parent is the only serious teacher the child has. Even after entering school and spending several hours of a day, five days a week, with his teacher, the child's main teachers are still his parents. The parents continue to spend a lot more time with the child, and have already developed an in-depth relationship that no one, short of a marriage partner, will duplicate. Therefore, a tremendous amount of instruction in attitudes, values, conscience, relationships, responsibilities, problem solving, etc., has already been absorbed, and these qualities are rapidly on their way to becoming an integral part of this child's personality and internalized life pattern.[3]

Many times a child will show up doing something or acting out something the parent does, and the parent expresses surprise. The parent will say, "But I never told him that!" Actually, the parent has communicated something, though not verbally—rather by his or her actions and attitudes. Remember, in any close relationship, *other forms of communication become far more important than words themselves.* Communication comes in many forms as follows:

> look in our eyes
> tone of voice
> body language

actions
distance we keep
touch
feelings we transmit from within

All of these become primary forms of teaching and communicating which the child observes and absorbs.

An example from the Old Testament character of Abraham and his posterity helps us to see this principle at work. It also helps us to further understand Exodus 34:7 which says, "He [God] does not leave the guilty unpunished; he punishes the children and their children for the sin of the fathers to the third and fourth generation." The Hebrew word iniquity in this verse actually means "bend, twist, distort, or pervert." Thus, this passage is saying that God is visiting the *bents, twistings, distortions,* and *perversions* of the fathers unto the children of the third and fourth generation.[4]

Note from the life of the Old Testament character Abraham: Abraham had the habit of lying when he felt the end justified the means. In Genesis 12:10-13, Abraham had to go down to Egypt because of a severe famine. He was fearful that others would see the beauty of his wife, Sarah, and kill him in order to have her. He therefore instructed her to say that she was his sister.

Later on, in a similar situation but in a different country, Abraham repeated this same pattern. Sarah was again to be known as his sister in order that Abraham himself might escape injury. The plot was found out in each case and failed to work as Abraham had planned.

Note that Abraham's son Isaac, in the account in Genesis 26:6, 7, repeated exactly the same lie in instructing his wife Rebekah to be known as his sister in order that he might relieve his own anxiety about the possibility of being killed because of her. Again, this plot did not work out as he had planned, but the bent for lying was definitely there. He learned it by observing his father.

Isaac's son was named Jacob, which meant "supplanter" or "deceiver." He had a nasty habit of deception and used it beautifully in order to gain things for himself. He deceived his brother, Esau, into giving up his birthright. This amounted to a double portion of the inheritance from his father, which normally went to the eldest son. He also lied to his dying father so that he might receive the greatest part of the blessing from him. The same trait that began with Abraham was passed on to Isaac, and then passed on to Jacob.

Note also Jacob's sons. Because of their jealousy toward their brother Joseph, they conceived a plot together. They captured Joseph, sold him into slavery, and took his coat of many colors and dipped it into animal blood. They then brought the coat to Jacob and *lied* to their father, saying that Joseph had been accidentally killed by an animal and was no longer alive. Again, we see that the bent toward lying continues on, unchecked.[5]

And where does it stop? We can see that the values of the parents, good and bad, are passed to the children, who in turn pass them on to their children, and so on.

Looking at Ourselves

From these examples, we can see that it's very important for each of us as parents to examine our own lives, intentions, attitudes, values, and ways of doing things very carefully. We should work daily on our own personal growth in order that our children learn from us in the right way, and in turn will be able to instruct their children correctly.

As architects of the family unit, it would be well worth it for the husband and wife to evaluate their own relationship together, and thus seek a firm foundation stone for the family unit. The following descriptive adjectives may be helpful for each parent in evaluating his own personal relationship with his spouse:

warm and affectionate	*vs.*	*indifferent*
supportive	*vs.*	*undermining*
thoughtful and caring for others	*vs.*	*self-centered*
accepting, able to give praise	*vs.*	*critical and rejecting*

spontaneous	vs.	inhibited
humble	vs.	proud
giving	vs.	grasping
argumentative	vs.	able to discuss opinions thoughtfully
demanding own way	vs.	able to bend and compromise
closed, covert communicator	vs.	open to direct communication
lying and deceitful	vs.	transparently honest
mistrustful	vs.	trustful
avoids responsibility	vs.	takes responsibility seriously in solving problems
two separate individuals	vs.	ability to work as a team
too busy	vs.	have time for each other

A husband and wife communicate these values to each other by their own actions, the children will in turn observe and learn the same values, and will strongly tend to act them out in their own marriage and family relations in years to come.

A word of caution is in order at this point. A parent could conclude from all that has been said up to this point, that everything his child becomes, both good and bad, is directly his fault, and that nothing can be done to change it. The grandchildren will simply be more of the same. Depressing, right? But there are other factors that enter into the total picture. Many of these will be explained later in this series, but a few are worth mentioning here.

First, kids vary widely within the same family in some of their characteristics, simply because they are born with different personalities and temperaments to start with, and thus react differently. Second, each child has a will and, to some degree, may choose a different life style than that of the parents, depending somewhat on his or her own self-understanding and basic determination to be different. Third, there may be other factors at birth which affect the outcome of the child, of which the parent has no control, such as: birth defects, disease of genetic origins, biological influences on behavior, etc. Fourth, environmental factors may influence the outcome. For instance, a teenager from a good home may fall in with the wrong crowd and get into trouble. This is not always controllable by parents. Fifth, God is just as interested in the growth of our children as we are—even more so. And he has stated that he is at work in each of them to accomplish things that no parent can accomplish.[6] Sixth, as you grow, your kids will grow, and thus they are not locked into the present problem areas within the family.

Do your part, and God will do his. The rest is the responsibility of your child in his or her adult years.

Workbook Section Chapter Two

1. *My relationships to my family.*

In the spaces below, write down the things you do for your kids on the left. Write down the things you do for your spouse on the right. Use short phrases.

Kids   Spouse

_____   _____
_____   _____
_____   _____
_____   _____
_____   _____
_____   _____
_____   _____
_____   _____
_____   _____
_____   _____
_____   _____
_____   _____

Try honestly to rate the urgency that you put on each item on a scale of 1 to 10, with 10 being very urgent, and 1 not urgent at all. Put the numbers in the margin.

Now add up the numbers on each side. This will give you some idea of who gets the most attention, your kids or your spouse. Does this give you any idea as to where your relationship is stronger?

2. *Family relationship triangle.*

Draw the triangle of relationships that best fits the description of your relationships with your spouse and with each of your kids, as illustrated on pages 21, 22, and 23 of the text.

H   W   H   W   H   W

C1   C2   C3

Is there anything you would like to change in the balance of these relationships? Write down what you see:

_____
_____
_____

Write down what you would like to change:

_____
_____
_____

3. *Evaluation of relationship characteristics.*

Rate yourself on the list of characteristics in relation to your spouse. Use the following rating system on yourself:

E-excellent   G-good   A-average   P-poor   H-help!

Your view of yourself		Your spouse's view of you
E G (A) P H	warm and affectionate vs. indifferent	E (G) A P H
E (G) A P H	supportive vs. undermining	E (G) A P H
E (G) A P H	thoughtful and caring vs. self-controlled	E G (A) P H
E G (A) P H	accepting, can give praise vs. critical and rejecting	E (G) A P H
E G (A) P H	spontaneous vs. inhibited	E G A (P) H

E G (A) P H	humble	vs. proud	E G (A) P H
E G (A) P H	giving	vs. grasping	E (G) A P H
E (G) A P H	can discuss openly and thoughtfully	vs. argumentative	E G (A) P H
E (G) A P H	can bend or compromise	vs. must have own way	E (G) A P H
E G (A) P H	open, direct in communication	vs. closed, covert in communication	E G (A) P H
E G (A) P H	transparently honest	vs. lying, deceitful	(E) G A P H
(E) G A P H	trusting	vs. mistrustful	(E) G A P H
E G (A) P H	responsible in problem solving	vs. irresponsible	E (G) A P H
E (G) A P H	work as a team	vs. individualistic	E (G) A P H
E G A (P) H	makes time for the other	vs. too busy	E G A (P) H

Go through the list again and try to answer *as you think your spouse would describe you.*

Discuss with your spouse how he or she actually sees you.

4. *Things to change.*

Write two things you would like to change within yourself in the *immediate* future. _____

_____

Long range: List five things you would like to change within yourself during the next *twelve months.* ____

_____

_____

_____

Jot down one thing you are willing to commit yourself to work on every day for the next week. _____

_____

Pray about it daily. Begin each day committed to God, seeking his help to make some measurable progress, such as, "I insisted on my own way only twice, instead of five times, this week."

[1]Virginia Satir, *Conjoint Family Therapy* (Palo Alto, Cal.: Science and Behavior Books, Inc., 1967), p. 2.

[2]*Ibid.*, pp. 4, 5.

[3]*Ibid.*, p. 27.

[4]Charles R. Swindoll, *You and Your Child* (New York: Thomas Nelson, Inc., 1977), pp. 35, 36.

[5]*Ibid.*, pp. 37-43.

[6]Ephesians 1:6.

Three
Parental Roles

There are several models which may serve as patterns for the parental role. A few are given in the following paragraphs:

1. *The architect.* The architect has a certain concept in his mind of a building that he wishes to create. He then attempts to translate that mental image to initial sketches, drawings, and later to blueprint specifications and instructions. The blueprints will be used to build and complete that structure in sufficient detail to make it the realization of the architect's original idea. He is a designer.

2. *The coach.* The coach takes a group of somewhat talented but untrained people into discipline, instruction, hardening exercises, strategy sessions, correction, and encouragement and seeks to shape them into a team capable of competition with similar teams. He exposes them to the rough and tumble, allows them to experience a few mistakes, and helps them learn from these experiences. He is a trainer.

3. *The teacher.* The teacher has certain goals that he wishes his children to obtain. Through planning, through specific instruction, exercises, discipline, and encouragement, he seeks to help his child reach these stated goals. He is an instructor.

A new parent soon begins to realize there's far more required than simply speech giving, a few words of advice, or occasional punishment for misbehavior. Parenting is a long-range process to lead a child through many developmental milestones to reach the goal of responsible adult behavior and achievement. There are numerous specific steps along the way to help you reach that final goal.

Ways of Training

How does a parent go about training his child, coaching him, designing and building a life? There are several very important ingredients that require the active participation of each parent.

Example

The most powerful method of teaching of all is the example of what each parent does, what he says, how he does it, and the attitudes that accompany what he says and does. The child is securing a tremendous amount of information and data just from *observing* his parents.

The following are some examples of things the child observes and learns from parental example:

> dodging problems or meeting them head on
> open and honest communication or indirect, deceitful communication
> responsibility taken seriously or lackadaisically
> adherence to rules of right and wrong, or rules bent whenever there is opportunity
> open expression of affection or cold indifference
> avoidance of conflict, or the ability to defend oneself when necessary
> sharing with others, or selfish, greedy, jealous, possessive attitudes
> flexible and adaptable or rigid and unbending
> dominating and overbearing, passive and retiring, or assertive and appropriately forward

In growing up, the child does not question whether the parent is doing right or wrong, but simply accepts that this is the way things are done in life. He has no other comparison for he is too young, undeveloped, and dependent to seriously question his parents' actions. In teenage years, he may begin to compare his parents with other parents and raise some questions, but by that time, a great deal of what he has learned is already part and parcel of his personality. He will either tend to grow according to the example his parents have given him or try to be the opposite in some ways. He'll either join it or fight it. In a few short years, he will have internalized his own values, good and bad, right and wrong, either accepting or rejecting parental example and action.

The main lesson is that *parents are teaching by example all of the time,* even when they say nothing, express no opinions, and give no verbal clues. The child still picks up on their intentions and integrates this into his own personality.

Teaching Responsibility

By the time the parent realizes that his child chronically leaves behind him a well-blazed trail of toys, books, crayons, nuts and bolts, and "you name it, you got it," the parent concludes, "something is missing." In fact, if the parent says nothing, he or she will find himself constantly following the well-marked trail as the main "picker upper," realizing the missing link is something called a sense of responsibility.

Children have to be taught that life is not all play. They need specific instruction in picking up toys they have brought out, straightening messes they have made, mending books they have torn, washing crayon off the walls which they have decorated, etc.

A very young child needs a lot of play time. An adult also needs some play time, but not in nearly the same proportion. A child needs a gradual but steady introduction to the fact that there is work as well as play; to be done. When he is old enough he needs to be taught how to take on a few chores around the house, such as helping with the dishes, setting the table, cleaning his room, helping with the trash, and doing other odd jobs. This again is part of the twenty-year process, with the amount of work increasing and the amount of play decreasing, but never completely disappearing. Note the accompanying diagram:

What happens if a child is never taught adult responsibilities, and has all play and no work? The result will be: carousing, low academic achievement, probably delinquency and unpreparedness for the adult world. He will be a lazy, spoiled, undisciplined brat.

What happens if the child is taught all work and no play? The child will grow up old before his time, become

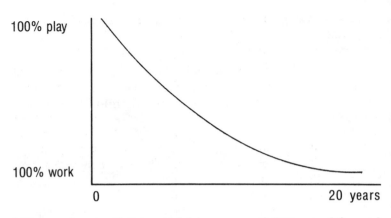

100% play

100% work

0   20 years

bitter and resentful toward his responsibilities in life, and probably experience a period of "having his fling" at a later time when it's quite inappropriate to his situation in life.

Note this principle carefully: The *primary motive* for giving chores to children is *not* to relieve the parents of work, but to *prepare the children for life in the working world ahead of them.*

Specific Instruction

Specific instruction can be practiced in a number of different ways. Several of these are discussed in the following paragraphs:

1. *Show how to do things.* Although you could undoubtedly do a task yourself much faster and easier, take the time to demonstrate how it is to be accomplished, and the result you desire. Be specific. Do not give orders without demonstrating ways they are to be carried out and their degree of thoroughness. Don't leave your child with vague instructions and then subject him to criticism for failure to read your mind. Be clear, concise, and patient. Work with the child the first few times to help him get the idea.

2. *Teach through consistent requirements.* Requirements that change, according to how you feel at that moment, only serve to confuse the child and make him feel unsure of himself in your presence. Think through first of all what you want to be accomplished, and how, and then make real efforts to state all of this clearly. If you've made a mistake, acknowledge it openly and show how it can be cor-

rected. The main purpose here is to help the child learn to organize himself in order to accomplish what he needs to accomplish. This will require time and effort by the parent.[1]

3. *Teach values in life.* A child is not born with an inherent sense of what is right and wrong. This comes through teaching and training. Take the time to teach your child the things that are important in life. This should include not only *moral values* (what is *right* and what is *wrong*), but also the values of the *good*, the *beautiful*, and the *desirable*. For example, a child needs to be taught that it is wrong to lie, steal, inflict needless pain upon another, or take advantage of the weakness of another, etc.

A child also needs to be taught the *values of truthfulness* and *honesty* as the foundation for trust and deeper personal relationships. There is nothing more damaging to a personal relationship than chronic lying and deception in other forms. Dishonesty creates a cancerous growth of distrust which in turn leads to protective withdrawal and distance from others. Require truthfulness from your children, and punish for lying. Give direct answers to their questions and carry out the promises that you have made. Teach them the value of helping others in need, and the art of self-defense when appropriate. Teach them creativity and the value of appropriate self-expression.[2] Creativity is fostered by an environment that is not overly restrictive, but in which the child is encouraged to experiment with different things — one in which mistakes are not a disaster, but a learning tool for the next try.

4. *Teach basic modesty.* Help children to know when their dress and appearance is appropriate and when it is not. Help guide them in their choices of entertainment, and in choosing that which is appropriate for them. Teach them how to handle the overstimulation of various news and advertising media, as well as life itself. Teach them the proper place of sex in life, and the appropriate expression of love, as well as the inappropriate.

5. *Set reasonable rules.* A child with no firm rules is basically a deprived child. He will be lazy and undisciplined because he has undisciplined parents who basically dropped out of that role in life themselves. He will be quite

unprepared for responsibility and self-discipline in adult life.[3]

Here are some basics that parents should insist on:

1. Knowing where your kids are.
2. Knowing your kid's friends, and the kind of influence they wield.
3. Only limited amounts given in money, with a requirement to earn the rest for themselves.
4. A few definite jobs around the house.
5. Basic neatness.
6. Respect for parental authority which extends to other authority.
7. Respect toward others of his own age.

A child needs specific instruction in each area.

Punishment as a Teaching Method

God makes it clear that the father is head of the home and is held directly responsible for that task. Ephesians 6:4 states, "Fathers, do not exasperate your children; instead, bring them up in the training and instruction of the Lord." Proverbs 4:3, 4 states, "When I was a boy in my father's house, still tender, and an only child of my mother, he taught me and said, 'Lay hold of my words with all your heart; keep my commands and you will live.' " The father is given the main responsibility of the task.

Obedience is not just something to be preferred or desired. Obedience is something to be *required*, from God's point of view. A child does not naturally follow the way he should go. Definite effort is required on the part of the parents. Proverbs 22:15 states, "Folly is bound up in the heart of a child, but the rod of discipline will drive it far from him." Note the words: folly or foolishness is bound in the heart of the child. He is not naturally wise and good, but will naturally follow the wrong way, if left to himself. Note also that the way of getting rid of the foolishness is through *the rod of discipline*. The father who neglects this aspect of teaching will bring about just the opposite, as expressed in Proverbs 19:13, "A foolish son is his father's ruin." The father must back up his teaching with appropriate discipline.

Teaching must be backed up with consequences. Education of the public about speed limits on our highways should be supported by the reasoning that overspeeding only creates more accidents, more people lose their lives, and resources of gasoline energy are wasted. Thus speeding actually accomplishes very little in itself. A change in people's driving habits is accomplished by the high visibility of men in white cars with flashing red lights who have and use the authority to fine violators. Did you ever notice how everyone suddenly slows down to the speed limit when a police car is in view? This simply demonstrates that instruction, without necessary discipline to back it up, produces inadequate results. The presence of disciplinary authority brings obedience.

Take the example of the mother who has for the fifteenth time screamed, "This is the last time I'm going to tell you." The child indifferently goes on doing exactly what he's been doing for the last fourteen dramatizations, knowing that no action is really called for until one can be sure that Mother really means business. Threats, with no action, produce indifference in children, tuning out what they don't want to hear, and providing entertainment by the desperate antics of the frustrated parent.

Trying to please a child and to win his favor by giving in when he carries on and on, pleases no one, and accomplishes nothing but *frustration*. The child, then, grows up to learn only how to manipulate and to blame his parents for their lack of backbone.

Back up the instruction with firmness. When you say, "This is the last time I'm going to tell you," it had better be the last time, and some definitive action needs to follow if the child does not respond. Every child needs to learn that there are consequences for bad behavior and rewards for good behavior. The knowledge of these is as vital as life and breath.

Clinical experience indicates that *kids want rules!* (Don't faint, Mom.) Many a parent has thought that by giving in, he has shown the child his love. Quite the contrary. Instead, the child complains, "My parents don't love me."

When asked, "Why?" they respond, "They don't make me follow any rules." Children know, deep within themselves, that they are unable to direct their own lives without some outside help, and they want their parents to provide that structure for them. Parents who do not provide it, for whatever reason, are giving the message that they don't care enough to teach the children what they need to learn.[4]

What is the main motivation for using punishment to correct children? The main motivation is *not* the parent's own anger or annoyance at the child. The main reason for discipline is *to correct behavior* that needs correction, not only for the moment, but also for the future. The goal is to bring up a child who understands right from wrong, who had learned adequate self-control to regulate his own life within reasonable standards. The parent will use various means to help the child obtain these goals, including punishment, when that is appropriate. The parent's own personal comfort and ease is *not* the primary motive, rather the punishment is for *the child's long-range welfare.*

Actually, it should be said that the use of spanking is only one of several ways of changing behavior, or of driving foolishness away from the child. The Hebrew word that is translated "rod" in several passages in Proverbs in reference to punishment of children is used in several ways in Scripture. It can refer to a rod used in corporal punishment, but is also used to refer to the shepherd's staff that is used to gather his sheep, and also the scepter or sign of authority of an ancient ruler.[5]

The emphasis is upon the *authority* that the rod represents and the proper use of that authority.

Consider also the fact that not all kids respond well to the same form of enforcement. Some are very sensitive and compliant, and all they need is that certain "look" from the parent, and obedience follows. A physical spanking for this child would only crush the inner spirit. There are other kids who seem completely unaffected by all the spankings a parent can possibly provide, and even laugh at the frustrated parent in his futility. For this child, isolation in his or her room may turn out to be the most effective weapon. For others, a few well-timed spankings, with the visibility of the rod as the sign of authority (in combination with other teaching methods) may accomplish the job well.

Whatever method proves the most effective, that's the one to use. Other methods of motivation to proper behavior will be considered in later chapters, but the main message is clear. *The parent is directly responsible for the correction, training, and teaching of the child.* No one else has this primary task.

The Word of God makes it clear that a parent who abdicates this responsibility is tampering with a divine order. Proverbs 29:15 states, "The rod of correction imparts wisdom, but a child left to himself disgraces his mother." Verse 17 further states, "Discipline your son and he will give you peace; he will bring delight to your soul." To say it another way, the rod of correction drives away foolishness, brings wisdom and maturity to the child, who in turn later will bring delight to his parents as they see the rewards of their efforts.

"The father of a righteous man has great joy; he who has a wise son delights in him" (Prov. 23:24).

Training through Love

As parents, look for ways to grow closer to your children. Children want very much to have some companionship with their parents and will crave it one way or another. If they cannot get their parents' attention in a good way, they may well choose to do the wrong things in order to be noticed. After all, to get some attention, even for being naughty, is better than to get no attention at all. It is better to be hollered at than to be ignored. To put it another way, to have bad breath is better than to have no breath at all.

The following paragraphs give some specific steps that can be taken to help build that atmosphere of love and caring that is so vital to the child's sense of importance and growth:

1. *Spend time with your children.* Roughhousing with Father, baking with Mother, storytime, a few good television shows, some games all shared together mean a great deal to children. Parents may be afraid to give time to their

children for fear the children will want all of it. Basically, this is not true. Some definite time planned for your children that is specifically *their* time, is usually sufficient; then they are quite content to busy themselves with other things. Thirty minutes a day spent with your children will mean more than you can ever begin to realize.

2. *Make your home the center of your child's happiness.* It is not necessary for a parent to buy expensive things or provide expensive entertainment to find happiness. Some of the greatest times that children cherish and remember with the most warmth are simple picnics in the park, when their parents took time to play games with them and do what they wanted, which may not have cost a single dime. Somehow they remember these events even more than a bundle of money spent in an amusement park, as important as such an outing may be to them.

3. *Include your children in your activities.* Headed downtown on an errand? Invite them to go along. If you like to fish, invite them too. If you are building something as a project, invite them to help, when appropriate. If not appropriate, give them a hammer, some nails, and some scraps of material and let them do their own construction job, right alongside of you. One cardinal truth is that time is of far more value than material possessions, as far as relating to children is concerned. *No material possession, no matter how valuable, can replace the importance of time you spent with your children.*[6]

4. *Give sincere compliments whenever possible.* Look for any new efforts or new ability to accomplish things important to the child. Let the child know that you are aware of this, and that you are happy he is trying to do things. A simple word here and there will do far more to spur further constructive efforts than a thousand lectures or restraints could ever do.

Love is many little things all wrapped up together. It is such things as: listening, a moment shared, a hug on the run, a ride in the country, an afternoon at the beach, a song at the supper table, a compliment, dropping your magazine to listen, ruffling of the hair, wiping away a tear, and encouragement to do better tomorrow.[7] It's all of these and more.

Individual Roles of Father and Mother

Most of the things that parents will do for their children will be as a team effort, father and mother working together toward common goals for their children. However, there are certain distinctive roles for which each parent is responsible.

Father Role

Ephesians 6:4 has some specific instructions for the father: "Fathers, do not provoke your children to anger, but bring them up in the discipline and instruction of the Lord" (RSV). Thus in God's divine order, there are two specific responsibilities for the father.

1. He is designated the head of the home in this passage, and in Ephesians 5, which deals with the husband and wife roles for the home. He is directly responsible for the training and discipline of his children.
2. In carrying out that discipline, he is to be careful to avoid provoking or exasperating his children to anger. Thus, as head of the home, he is to *avoid extremes.*

It would be easy for the father to become the *tyrant,* the king of the mountain, "Do as I say, or else." He would then be treating his children as though he were a dictator, with them as his slaves and obedient servants. The chance for open discussion and real sensitivity to the individual child and his specific needs would be missing. The other extreme is for the father to become so *passive* that he would, in essence, be saying, "Do whatever you want." Either of these extremes brings *resentment* and *exasperation* to the heart of a child. Many a child has made it clear in counseling sessions that he wants a parent who is *loving* and *fair,* but who also requires *responsibility* and *reasonable obedience.*

This does not mean that the father, as head of the home, does everything. It simply means that he is responsible for the overall operation of the family, and the overall guidance of his children. He may very well delegate a lot of this responsibility to the mother, and will definitely invite her input, experience, and judgment in every situation. The president of a company who carries on his business wisely does not attempt to make every decision completely on his own, or do everything for himself. He knows how to delegate authority, how to get things done through other people, how to invite the expertise of others who may be more knowledgeable in certain specific areas, and to use all this information in his final judgments. However, the buck has to stop somewhere, and he alone is responsible for the final outcome, even though he did not do all the work. He enlists the help of qualified others.

Thus we can say that the father of the home is responsible for initiating the policies and directions of the family system. He is responsible for maintaining the policies in that direction, and to see that they are carried out on a day-to-day, week-to-week, and year-to-year basis. The father is responsible for the final outcome of the family. He takes the leadership in teaching the values, obedience, love, and spiritual responsibilities of each individual. He does not do every part of it.

In the Ten Commandments, God places the responsibility directly upon the parents for the teaching of his law. Deuteronomy 6:6-9 says:

> These commandments that I give you today are to be upon your hearts. Impress them on your children. Talk about them when you sit at home and when you walk along the road, when you lie down and when you get up. Tie them as symbols on your hands and bind them on your foreheads. Write them on the doorframes of your houses and on your gates.

The main responsibility for the teaching of these spiritual values was placed upon the father.[8]

Mother Role
The mother's role is to be basically supportive of the father's leadership, and to play a very large part in the

total upbringing of the children. There will be areas in which she has more expertise than the father, and by working together as a team, each using his respective abilities, they will together fulfill their goals with their children.

The mother may have more time and patience in such things as help with homework, listening to their problems, working out difficulties with playmates, showing compassion and comfort when hurt, or administering discipline when the father is absent. She will do better at teaching certain skills such as cooking, sewing, etc. The mother should use her talents with her children as her part of the total ministry.

As more and more mothers work outside the home, it becomes increasingly important for the mother and father to sit down together and work out a sharing of responsibility. For the mother to be expected not only to work full time, but also to clean the house, wash the clothes, cook the meals, and carry the major burden of raising the children with their many little problems—while the husband carries only a few things besides his job—is just not realistic. The mother is just as entitled to relaxation as the father, and is not to be viewed as his servant, while the father sits around doing little.

There will be times when it becomes difficult for the mother to support the father's action as well as times when the father does not agree with the mother's way of handling matters. Many of these problems are better worked out together privately to avoid the problem of the child playing one against the other, or one parent undermining the authority of the other. The parents may need to call "time out" from the problem at hand to confer with one another, and come to a joint decision. This does not mean that there can never be a disagreement of the mother and father in front of their children, as these are inevitable. Indeed, there are times when differing views need to be discussed in front of the children, with combined effort toward reaching a solution. This is a valuable teaching tool for children to learn how to resolve conflict that will prepare them for such difficulties in later years. The unity of the home and the solidarity of the parents must be kept in view. Discretion must dictate when one approach is preferable to another. Too much conflict produces insecurity in children.

The Father and Mother Relationship

The greatest gift that any parents can give to their children is the demonstration of their affection, loyalty, trust, compassion, acceptance, and understanding of each other. A family in which the father and mother are sincerely in love with each other provides the following:

1. A secure home in which the children feel safe, wanted, and loved.
2. Instruction by example for future adulthood and marriage roles to the children. As the parents solve their problems together, express affection in little important ways, and basically "show how it is done" the children are receiving tremendously valuable training for their own future families.
3. Training specifically in what husbands and wives do, and how they act in their respective roles. The children get a free home demonstration as to what fathers do as head of the family, and what mothers do in their role in the family.
4. Affection. What draws children to their father and mother quicker than anything? When father and mother are hugging each other. All want to join in; even the dog wants to get into the act.

The following two equations illustrate an important point:

Unity + love = secure children, well prepared for life.

Disunity + excessive conflict = insecure children, poorly prepared for life.

Workbook Section Chapter Three

1. Methods of teaching.

Out of these three teaching methods: example, specific instruction, and love:

    a. Which do you do best? _____

       How could you further improve? _____

    b. Which do you do the worst? _____

       How could you further improve? _____

2. Teaching by example.

List the areas where you are:

A poor example   A good example

_____   _____

_____   _____

_____   _____

_____   _____

_____   _____

3. Specific instructions.

    a. I take time to show my kids how to:

_____

_____

_____

    b. Some things I want to teach my kids how to do for themselves in the next three months are: (list) _____

_____

_____

_____

_____

4. *Spiritual emphasis.*

Some ways I could improve the spiritual emphasis in our home are: (list) _____

_____

_____

_____

5. *Father and mother specialties.*

In training our kids, I find there are certain areas where:

I do better	My spouse does better
_____	_____
_____	_____
_____	_____
_____	_____
_____	_____

6. *Father and mother roles.*

In the following list of statements, circle the number which represents your view.

(1) strongly agree   (3) not sure   (5)strongly disagree
(2) mildly agree   (4) mildly disagree

Wife		Husband
1 (2) 3 4 5	The husband is the head of the home.	1 2 3 4 (5)
1 2 3 4 (5)	The wife should not be employed outside of the home.	1 2 (3) 4 5
1 2 3 (4) 5	The husband should help regularly with the dishes.	1 (2) 3 4 5
1 2 3 4 (5)	The wife has the greater responsibility for the children.	1 2 3 4 (5)
1 2 3 4 (5)	The wife should always be the one to cook.	1 2 3 4 (5)
1 2 3 4 (5)	Major decisions should be made by the husband in case of an impasse.	1 2 3 4 (5)
(1) 2 3 4 5	The husband and wife should plan the budget and manage money matters together.	1 2 (3) 4 5
1 2 3 (4) 5	The father is the one responsible for disciplining the children.	1 2 3 4 (5)
1 (2) 3 4 5	A wife who has a special talent should have a career.	1 2 (3) 4 5

1 2 3 4 5	Arguments are a definite part of marriage.	1 2 3 4 5
1 2 3 4 5	The wife is just as responsible for the children's discipline as the husband.	1 2 3 4 5
1 2 3 4 5	It is the husband's job to do yardwork.	1 2 3 4 5
1 2 3 4 5	The mother should be the teacher of values to the children.	1 2 3 4 5
1 2 3 4 5	Children should be allowed to help plan family activities.	1 2 3 4 5
1 2 3 4 5	Children develop better in a home with parents who are strict disciplinarians.	1 2 3 4 5
1 2 3 4 5	The wife should always obey what her husband asks her to do.	1 2 3 4 5
1 2 3 4 5	The husband should decide which areas each should be responsible for.	1 2 3 4 5
1 2 3 4 5	The husband's responsibility is to his job and the wife's is to the home and children.[9]	1 2 3 4 5

After you have completed your answers, have your spouse fill out the same set of statements. Compare your results together, discuss them, and seek to work out some reasonable solutions to your differing views.

[1]Larry Christiansen, *The Christian Family* (Minneapolis, Minn.: Bethany Fellowship, 1970), p. 68.

[2]*Ibid.*, pp. 74, 75.

[3]*Ibid.*, pp. 78, 79.

[4]*Ibid.*, p. 94.

[5]Francis Brown, S. R. Driver and Charles A. Briggs, *A Hebrew and English Lexicon* (London: Oxford University Press, 1952), pp. 986, 987.

[6]Christiansen, pp. 122, 123.

[7]*Ibid.*, p. 125.

[8]See 1 Samuel 3:11-14, where God holds Eli directly responsible for his sons' behavior, for not restraining and correcting them.

[9]Adapted from the book by Norman Wright, *The Christian Faces . . . Emotions, Marriage and Family Relationships* (Denver: Christian Marriage Enrichment, 1975), p. 113.

Four
The Right Ingredients

"I believe that kids should be made to do what they are told immediately, with no questions asked. They need to know who is in charge here."

"I think kids today need a lot of love, so I am going to give my kids all I can."

"Kids are a pain. They always want something. They're never satisfied. I'm too busy to be bothered with all of their petty complaints."

"Rules, that's what they need, more rules! These kids wander around getting into trouble because no one makes them toe the mark. No wonder they get into all kinds of problems."

"I'm confused. One expert is telling me one way to raise my children, and another expert is telling me another. Which one is right? I don't know what to do."

"My kids won't help me do anything. If I ask them to help with the dishes or rake the yard, I get all kinds of verbal abuse. I give up. If they want to be bums, let them be bums."

"I try to tell my kids what I expect out of them, but I like to encourage them by compliments when they do what I ask."

Most of us at some time in our lives have wanted to experiment with putting different kinds of ingredients together to see what kind of results we can produce. This ranges from young aspiring cooks who try different ingredients on Mother's shelves to see what they can make, to budding young scientists experimenting with their chemistry sets. Somewhere along the way we learn that in order to produce good results, we have to put together certain ingredients in the right proportions. For instance, what happens when you substitute salt for sugar? Yuk! Or if you put in three *tablespoons* of salt instead of three teaspoons. Ugh!

Our budding young scientist is fascinated by the fact that he can mix three chemicals together — charcoal, sulphur, and potassium nitrate — and produce a very interesting compound called gunpowder. If he just mixes these together loosely and sets fire to them, the expected results do not happen. He simply has a lot of sparklers flying, a miniature Fourth of July. However, if he takes the same ingredients and packs them tightly together in a closed container, *boom!* An explosion results and our young friend's curiosity is satisfied at this point, assuming of course that he still remains intact.

We fully expect to get something out of a soda machine if we put the right amount of money into it. And so our thinking goes.

As parents approach the task of parenthood they may feel somewhat like they are approaching a slot machine. It is almost like asking, "How many quarters do I have to put into this thing before I get the final payoff? Will I win or lose?" Some of the main questions are, "What do I have to put into parenting to get the right kind of results in my kids? What kind of formula is there? What are the ingredients? What do I need to do to get the process going? How do I keep the process going to produce end results? What are the unknown quantities that go into the formula: Parent + Kid + ? = Mature Adult?"

Different Ingredients

What are some of the different ingredients necessary to raising kids? There are many different views of how it is to be done:

1. *Rigid rules.* There are those who say that as parents you must exercise very definite control over your kid's behavior. "I demand immediate obedience," one parent will say. "If you step out of line, you will hear from me immediately." This parent is clearly the absolute authority

in the home, and the kids are taught not to question that authority. The rules are very clear and unbendable. For example, the child is to be in bed by nine o'clock, with no exceptions at any time. Five minutes beyond that time brings on a major thunderstorm. The rules are clearly outlined and total compliance is expected.

2. *Permissiveness.* In the permissive approach, there are a few basic rules and some definite structure, but the rules are not rigidly adhered to. They can be bent from time to time, and sometimes even broken altogether. The kids themselves are allowed a much larger share in decision making, and there is an atmosphere of freedom.

3. *Neglect.* There are those who let their kids grow up however they're going to grow up with very little direction from the parents themselves. The kids are allowed to make their own choices, to fend for themselves in most situations, and the parents do not get involved. The kids are allowed to do pretty much *what* they want to, *when* they want to. There is no specific responsibility or obedience required. The basic message to the child is, "Go away and don't bother me; go do your own thing."

4. *Love and support.* This approach says the main ingredient in raising kids is supportiveness. Look for the positive aspects in the child and encourage these. Give sincere compliments, words of encouragement, and an open display of affection with frequent assurance of love and caring. Love is demonstrated by parents making time for their kids—to talk with them, play with them, work together, and generally be their companions. Correction and discipline tend to be demonstrated more by persuasion and reasoning as compared with force. The parent will take time to explain things, will demonstrate how things are done, and will shy away from criticism and judgment for mistakes.

The Best Ingredients

Which of these ingredients works out the best? A statistical study was sponsored at the University of Minnesota by three Ph.D. psychologists, and their findings were presented in a theory paper to the National Council of Family Relations Theory Workshop in Portland, Oregon.[1] The questions used in the study were designed to reveal what kind of parents raise children who have the following characteristics: 1) Those with high self-worth and self-esteem who are basically happy with who they are; 2) those who have a capacity to conform to authority of others. They get along well with teachers, parents, bosses, supervisors, and all authority figures; 3) those who follow the religious beliefs of their parents; 4) those who identify with a counter-culture that runs opposite to conventional ideas of what is right and good. Some examples of these would be the drug culture, motorcycle gangs, communes, etc. The values chosen would be definitely in reaction to the parents' basic values.

This study dealt with a large sampling of hundreds of high school juniors and seniors throughout the United States. The study cut across racial and cultural lines. A study of this design, nature, and magnitude can thus produce some tremendously significant information.

What were the findings of the research team as to the most powerful factors through which parents influence children? The two most powerful ingredients were found to be parental *control* and *support*.

Control was defined as the ability of the parents to manage a child's behavior. Control can be carried out in a number of different ways. It can be done by force, simply because the parent is larger than the child and can beat him up. It can also be done by manipulation, such as, making a child feel guilty unless he goes along with what you want him to do. Another method involves establishing rather firm boundaries and providing healthy and acceptable choices and opportunities within which the child may grow. This is a more positive approach.

Support was defined as the ability to make the child feel loved. This, of course, involves much more than simply telling the child you love him. It involves such things as inviting your children to sit on your lap. It involves kissing, patting, holding them close to you. It includes everyday communications of supportiveness, both spoken and unspoken, that convey to the child the sense that he is loved and cared for.

The Magic Recipe

Having discovered the two vital ingredients of *control* and *support,* how do we put them together to get the best results? The study continued to show that there are basically *four* different types of parenting styles, depending on just how we put these ingredients together. The illustrations that follow give a picture of each of these styles, showing the combination of support and control in quadrant form.

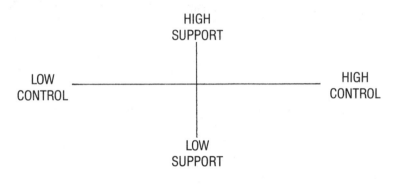

Illustration #1

Illustration #1 simply gives the empty quadrant to acquaint us with this type of illustration. Anything above the horizontal line indicates the degree of positive or high support, and anything below the horizontal line indicates negative, or lack of support. Anything to the right of the vertical line is positive or high control, and anything to the left of the vertical line is negative, or lack of control.

1. *Permissive parenting.* A permissive parent is *high in support* and *low in control.* There is a lot of warmth and caring, but obedience and responsibility are of lesser importance, though present. Note Illustration #2.

2. *Neglectful parenting.* The neglectful parent exercises *little control* and is *low in love* and *support.* This kind of parent basically lets the kids do what they want, requires few responsibilities, is not much concerned with obedience, and shows little personal warmth or caring in any outward form. Note Illustration #3.

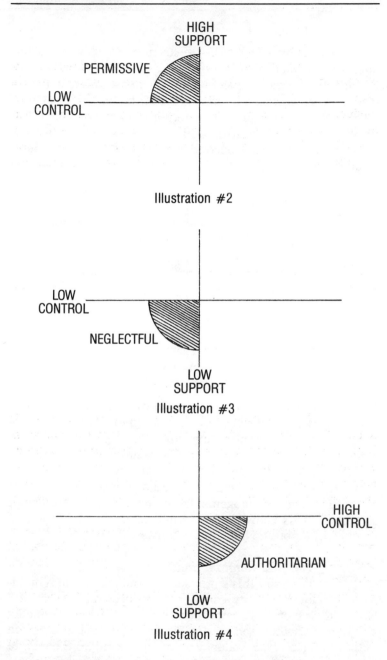

Illustration #2

Illustration #3

Illustration #4

3. *Authoritarian parenting.* Illustration #4 shows the authoritarian parent as very *high in control,* but quite *low in support.* This type of parent requires many rules, demands strict obedience with a lot of responsibility, but exercises very little positive expression of love, caring, or encouragement. The emphasis is on the negative, critical aspects of what the child does wrong with little encouragement when he does right. Note Illustration #4.

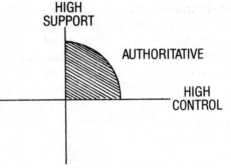

Illustration #5

4. *Authoritative parenting.* This sort of parenting is demonstrated by the parent who is *high in support* and *high in control.* This kind of a parent requires responsibility and obedience along with respect for authority. There are definite things for the child to carry out, and definite clear expectations for all of these. However, at the same time, there is also a great deal of love and caring, encouragement, and open display of affection so that the kids know they are cared for and loved beyond a shadow of a doubt. Note Illustration #5.

The Best Combination
What did this study show about the various combinations of love and control and what produced the best results? How did each of these parenting styles do as far as producing children with high self-worth, the ability to get along with authority figures, the tendency to follow the religious beliefs of their parents, as opposed to those who tend to rebel against parental values and join the ranks of a rebelling counterculture?

1. *Self-worth.* Children with the highest self-worth came from the homes of *authoritative parents* who had exercised a combination of *high support* and *high control.* This is convincing evidence that such a combination produces children with a *secure sense of self-respect.* Kids who scored second in this came from homes where parents were permissive, with low control but high support. Those from authoritarian homes with high control and low support came in third, while kids from the home of *neglectful parents* had the *lowest* rating.

2. *Conformity to authority.* Raising children who are able to conform and relate adequately to authority, the *authoritative parents* who had the combination of *high support* level and *high control,* scored the *highest.* The permissive parent with high support but low control again scored second. The neglectful parent, exhibiting low control and low support, came out third in this area, whereas the *authoritarian parent* who had high control but low support ranked the *lowest.*

3. *Religious values.* When it comes to children who most tend to accept their parents' faith and value system, again the *authoritative parent* with *high support* and *high control* scored the *best.* Also the permissive parent scored number two, and the neglectful parent number three, with the *authoritarian parent* the *lowest.*

4. *Identification with the counterculture.* The same study also brought out the types of homes that are most likely to produce kids who join countercultures such as hippie groups, communes, drug culture, motorcycle gangs, etc. It is interesting that both the *authoritarian* and the *neglectful* parents *tied* for *first place* in producing kids that went against their parental value system to join a very different system. The permissive parent scored next, while the *authoritative parent,* with high control and high support, again showed the *greatest success* with the *lowest* number of kids becoming involved in the counterculture.

Conclusions

These are not someone's opinions or some high sounding theory. These are the results of a scientific study based on the sound principles of statistical social research. The findings thus give valid data for seeing how these various combinations actually work out in real life.

Therefore, we can conclude from actual experience that the *best* combination of parental ingredients which will produce the happiest children—those most able to face life—will be: first of all, homes that have a good combination of *support* in the form of love, affection, and encouragement along with *parental control* in which the kids know what they are expected to do and do it. The *second best* parental style is that of permissiveness in which *high support* is given to kids, but also a lot *more leniency* as to requirements and rules. The *neglectful* and the *authoritarian* home tends to produce *problem kids* in all areas such as: low self-esteem, the ability to relate adequately to authority, carrying on the basic beliefs of their parents. These homes tend to produce the highest number of disrespectful, rebellious, and unruly kids. The combination of love and control in balance with one another provides an unbeatable combination. It's a winner!

Likewise, another interesting conclusion of this study is the fact that kids who know they are loved and cared for can manage with either high control or low control, and still come out reasonably well. However, *without love and caring and the feelings of belonging, they do not do well at all!*

Scriptural Parallels

The conclusions of these studies are very much in line with the teachings of Scripture. In Ephesians 6:4 parents are warned of overstrictness and rigidity with children. Children can be exasperated by abusive or neglectful parents to the point where they want nothing to do with the values and beliefs the parents represent. The clear warning to parents is to be careful not to antagonize your children, either by becoming overbearing, demanding, rigid and unbending, or by simply neglecting them and allowing them to fend for themselves when they are quite unprepared to do so.

The Scriptures are abundantly clear that God loves each of us who are born again into the family of God. The very familiar passage in John 3:16 tells us, "For God so loved the world that he gave his one and only Son, that whoever believes in him shall not perish but have eternal life." The *love* of the Father for each of us is clearly stated in numerous passages.

Scripture also presents *control* along with love, as a part of love. Proverbs 3:11, 12 tells us, "My son, do not despise the Lord's discipline and do not resent his rebuke, because the Lord disciplines those he loves, as a father the son he delights in." The New Testament picks up on the same theme, quoting from the same passage in Proverbs, and adding to it in Hebrews 12:10, 11.

> Our fathers disciplined us for a little while as they thought best; but God disciplines us for our good, that we may share in his holiness. No discipline seems pleasant at the time, but painful. Later on, however, it produces a harvest of righteousness and peace for those who have been trained by it.

God uses the combination of love and support along with discipline, training, and control. God encourages us with the assurance of his presence to help and guide us through the difficulties of life's journey. He shows us his love by accepting us as we are, not conditioning his love on strict obedience. He demonstrates his love by forgiving us, and gently restoring us when we go wrong. He also gives us definite principles of right and wrong to guide our lives. He gives us values to choose the most important things in life, and goals to work toward in our lives. When we go astray, God is right there to turn us back. He allows difficulty to come to us so that we might learn what is right and wrong, what values are good, and those that are empty illusions. He allows us to experience some difficulty that we might become stronger, and thus better able to meet the next test that life brings. *God is dedicated to our growth.* God expects us as parents to be dedicated to the growth and development of our children — to use similar principles. We will thus produce the kind of children we will be proud of.

The Wrong Ingredients

There is little question about the fact that parental *harshness* brings constant *humiliation* to the child. A rigid and icy atmosphere fosters constant fear in the child. He is thus taught that he is unable to make his own decisions, and his personality is squelched and stifled as a result. Therefore, instead of learning over the years to take an increasing amount of responsibility for his own life, this child faces life itself with fear, and severe dependency on others to tell him what to do.

Overwhelming hostility, bitterness, and even the possibility of psychosis may follow as a result.

Clinical practice also indicates that the child from the home in which he is neglected, given all kinds of freedom, and is shown little love also grows up with a tremendous amount of bitterness and hatred toward parents and other subsequent authority figures. This child also will be dependent, rebellious, and hostile because he has never been taught how to face life and take his responsibilities.

Noted psychologist James Dobson also points out one other problem of parental style that can later produce rather disastrous results. This is the home in which the father and mother present opposing extremes of love and control. The mother may be very lenient and permissive, and the father very strict and authoritarian. While the child is small, he may respond well to one parent while he is with that parent alone, and he may respond well to the other parent when he is with that parent alone. However, when he is with both parents together, he is confused and anxious, as he is not sure which way to follow. He becomes insecure and may become either hyperactive or may withdraw within himself as a result.

As the child grows, he eventually learns how to manipulate mother and father, setting them against each other to gain his own childish desires. If he is turned down by one parent, he may then present his request to the other parent to get what he wants. Once permission is received, the parents are left to fight it out with each other, while the kid walks away laughing up his sleeve at his victory. The result is that the child respects *neither* parent because each has undermined the authority of the other. The fuse is already lit on the time bomb of rebellion, and will surely explode in mushroom form at some point in adolescence. This is an important cause of extremely hostile and aggressive teenagers.[2]

Again, the principle of a balance of love and control must be sought by both parents, as a team working together in their joint responsibility from God, in order to produce healthy, responsible children (see below).

Love   Control

Illustration #6

Workbook Section Chapter Four

1. *Parental styles.*

Note each of the parental actions in the examples below, and determine: 1) What parenting approach is being used (authoritative, authoritarian, permissive, neglectful); 2) and what changes you would recommend.

    a. A father says to his fourteen-year-old daughter, "What do you mean by being late? Don't you know that it's five minutes after your time to be in? Some dependable kid you are. For this, you'll be grounded for the next four weeks!"

       Parenting type _____

       Recommended changes in approach _____

    b. Bobby, age four, is seated in the middle of a beautiful mud puddle, contentedly playing with his toy trucks. The mother, horrified, calls him to come out of the mud before he totally ruins his good clothes. Bobby ignores Mother's persuasion, and finally Mother gives up, saying, "Well, if you want to be a pig, just go ahead and be one. See if I care." She slams the door shut.

       Parenting style _____

       Recommended changes in approach _____

    c. Sally, age nine, wants to bake a cake in Mommy's kitchen. The mother says, "That sounds like fun. You know where things are; go ahead and enjoy yourself. If you have any problems, just let me know."

Parenting type _____

Recommended changes in approach _____

_____

_____

d. Billy, age eleven, wants to build a clubhouse in the backyard. He tells Dad of his intentions, to which the father replies, "I think that sounds like a good project. Let's go look for the best place to build it. Here is some wood you can start with, and when you need more, tell me. Remember that all tools you use must be returned and all messes cleaned up each evening. I know you will have a lot of fun, and it will be good experience for you."

Parenting type _____

Recommended changes in approach _____

_____

_____

2. *Self-evaluation.*

a. Some definite ways I expressed my love to my kids this past week are _____

_____

_____

b. Some definite ways I exercised control over my kids this past week are _____

_____

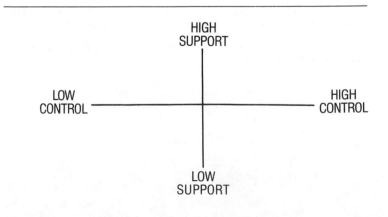

c. As I stop to think about it, my own parenting style fits that of the _____ parent, and can be drawn on the quadrant like this (draw on the diagram).

d. As I stop to think about it, I need to become stronger in the area of _____ , and to pull back in _____.

e. I am determined this week to work on _____

_____

_____

f. The ideal is to have a good balance of love and control.

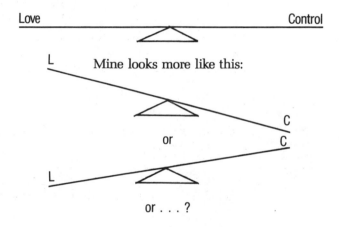

[1]Dennis Guernsey, "What Kind of Parent Are You?" *Family Life Today* (Glendale, Cal.: Gospel Light Publishers, 1975), I No. 2, pp. 8-10.

[2]James Dobson, *Dare to Discipline* (Wheaton, Ill.: Tyndale House Publishers, 1970), pp. 48, 49.

Five

Self-esteem — Under Construction

Nobody loves me,
everybody hates me,
I'm going out and eat worms.
Big fat juicy ones,
little tiny skinny ones,
my how they wiggle and they squirm.

The words to the little song introduce the national epidemic of our time, a low self-image. Like a contagious disease, the feeling of inferiority to others, being a second-class citizen, at the bottom of the totem pole, reaches everywhere to people in all situations. We compare ourselves with others. We somehow believe we have an incurable defect that is unacceptable to the society in which we live.

We are convinced that nobody likes us because:

I'm too short.
I'm too tall.
I'm too fat.
I'm too skinny.
I'm too dumb.
I'm too smart.
I have curly hair.
I have straight hair.
I have acne.
I have freckles.
I'm too poor.
I'm not a good player on the team.
I have thin legs.
I have fat legs.

All of the above are expressions of deep underlying feelings of inferiority.

Contributing Factors

There are a number of factors which contribute to a low self-image in the lives of our kids. Some of these come from society itself, in the everyday world we experience. We encounter them in radio, television, newspaper, advertising, and observe them in other people.

1. *Beauty*. One of the main values of our society held high before us is that of beauty. Note how people respond differently to a beautiful child than to a plain one. "My, aren't you a cute little gal . . . a handsome boy." At that point the child (not to mention the parents) swells with pride and confidence. But the "plain Jane" sister is wondering, "What's wrong with me?"

Comments such as this have a deep effect on the personality development of any child. He soon notes those who are popular, have plenty of friends, and are immediately accepted. These are the "haves," while he is one of the "have nots." For these beautiful "haves," things come easy. They don't have to work as hard, they naturally attract other beautiful people, and life seems to come easily to them.

Notice the emphasis of the media: "To be beautiful is happiness. Somewhat less than beautiful, even if it is a single visible flaw, is to be less than beautiful, and unhappy." Beauty becomes a god to be worshiped. None of these wonderful advertisements tells what it is like after beauty has faded and the person has to struggle like everyone else in the world.

2. *Intelligence*. People respond differently to a child who is obviously intelligent, than to the ordinary child. Average is never quite good enough. Note what happens when teams are picked for spelling contests in school. The appointed captains vie for those who are the brightest and quickest. The slower children are painfully aware of the fact that they are at the bottom of the pile, and will be the last to be chosen. They know clearly where they stand.

Note also in class recitation which ones the teachers obviously favor as they beam and smile. Clearly, the ones who are quick and have the correct answers. What child will ever forget the humiliating experience of having to do board work in front of the class, only to botch it up and receive disapproving comments from the teacher, as well as snickers and laughs from the kids in the class.[1]

3. *Materialism.* Status symbols of materialism are important to kids as well as to adults. The rich kids know who are the poor kids, and the poor kids know who are the rich kids. One boy says to another, "My father's rich. We're going to Europe this summer." The other boy is thinking about his occasional opportunity to swim in the dirty old river nearby. Another one says, "My dad just got a new car." The other fellow thinks about the outdated old clunker at home which runs on occasions, and wonders what's wrong with his family. The kid who is wearing hand-me-down clothes is very conscious of his status, compared to others with their finery. The ones who own an old black and white television know very well who has the new color television.

Peer Group Pressures

Other kids put unbelievable pressures on their peers. One of the ways is through intimidation by the stronger kids. The tough guys inflict terror and fear in the others. "Out of my way, kid." "Go home and cry to Mama." "Hey, faggot!" Frequently challenges and taunts make it clear who is superior and who is inferior.

There is also the severe pressure to conform to the group and to be the same as the others are. Anything out of the ordinary is taunted. Parents, who have finally felt relief in discovering that their child's poor performance is due to poor eyesight, have dutifully gotten glasses as the doctor prescribed. The child either refuses to wear them or loses them within the first week. Parents reprimand the child, but fail to realize the pressure of his peer group, which calls him "four eyes." "Only sissies wear glasses." The parent does not understand why his son gets extremely upset about a haircut, not realizing the tremendous amount of teasing he will take for it the next day at school. Anything that is *different* is considered "oddball."

The child who has to come in earlier than others,

or is restricted from certain places his friends may go, or required to accompany his parents when they go out, will receive the taunts of "still being tied to Mama's apron strings." The child then suffers untold humiliation from his peers and is challenged to somehow prove otherwise, in spite of his parents' expectations.

Name calling has never ceased. Words like: "Dumbo, radio ears, retarded, Bugs Bunny, fatso, stringbean, pimples," etc., all illustrate the frequent attacks of kids on others. Equally hard to manage are attacks upon a child's parents by his peers, such as: "Your old man couldn't find his way out of a paper bag." The jeers are very hard to take.

Parental Pressure

Parents are the primary influence on the child's self-esteem from day one, long before he is aware of peer group relationships or demands from society. Parents who know how to demonstrate love and warmth toward their newborn child, to respond to his needs in appropriate ways, instill in their child a sense of security, happiness, and self-worth. Even a tiny baby can sense the coldness, lack of compassion, and indifference from a parent who does not really love his child and resents his presence. The child becomes insecure and uncertain about himself and his own worth and value as a lovable individual.

Every child needs to develop a love relationship from the day he is born. A lack of this love relationship is the root cause for many serious emotional and mental problems in years to come. The very first year is fundamental to developing this sense of being somebody, and the basic effect lasts for a lifetime.[2] If the parent does not love the child and no one else consistently shows love, there is no way to discover his self-identity. The child who does not develop a self-identity from a secure love relationship is a prime candidate for serious emotional and mental illness in later years.[3]

1. *Conflicting messages.* Parents and children alike experience some confusion in the whole growing up process. No parent has ever fully understood how this perfect little angel can become such a little devil in such a short time, capable of driving the best of parents out of their skin.

Nor does a child who was once humored, considered cute and funny, fully understand the rejection, disapproval, and disgust he now receives for his wayward behavior.

As parents, we frequently give off conflicting messages to our children. For example, a mother may have no sooner finished telling her child how much she loves her, that she is more important to her than anyone in the whole world, than she walks off about her business. Suddenly her peaceful state is disrupted by a loud crash. She runs into the other room to see where a misguided ball has demolished her favorite lamp. "You stupid dummy!" The child is somewhat bewildered by his sudden reversal of approval.

Another child, having worked very hard, comes home with his report card and presents it to his father. After a period of silence, his father says, "Any dumbbell could do better than that." The child, deeply humiliated, turns and walks away discouraged.

Another conflicting message comes when we tell our children how important they are, but never have time to do anything with them. "I'm too busy, later." But somehow later never quite seems to get here.

Sarcastic humor presents another conflicting message. For example, "You're a fat tub . . . I was only kidding." Veiled humor does not ward off the darts that effectively find their targets in lowered self-esteem.

Conflicting messages in greater extremes produce the famous "double bind," so that whatever response the child chooses will be wrong and inadequate. The child easily sinks into the role of the "bad" guy of the family, to the point where he feels totally incapable of doing anything right.[4]

A few examples illustrate this principle. A father may tell his son quite clearly not to defy the parent's authority. At another time, the father taunts and challenges his son to take a swing at him to show he is a man. Either way he goes, the son will be wrong and is left to sort out his own confusion.

A mother carefully warns her daughter to "be very careful with boys" but proceeds to tell her daughter all the wild things she herself did to get them all worked up and aroused. Then the daughter is left with a double message, either to be very cautious in her times with boys, as the mother says, or to really drive them wild, as the mother did. The daughter is left to her own devices to sort this all out.

2. *Competitive messages.* Parents often give off a competitive message that seems to say, "I'm better than you will ever be." The parent always has to win at a game. "Ha! I beat you again!" Messages that the parent is always all-wise and will always be superior to the child contribute to further low self-esteem. "Why don't you ever grow up?" "Why can't you be like your sister? She always gets A's!" "You just can't manage your things." Such messages bring the kids into competition with each other and with their parents, with the resulting need to fight to the finish in order to win. The basic message they learn is to win at all costs. To lose is devastating, and to build a good relationship is irrelevant and doesn't matter.

3. *Rejection messages.* Our children are very vulnerable to even more direct messages of rejection. "I hate you!" "Drop dead, you creep!" "Go away, I'm too busy." "Get out of my life." All of these bring direct humiliation and self-hatred to the child, with a lot of hurt and anger that remains bottled up within throughout life. The child then views himself as a total failure and thus frustrates his own ability to achieve in the years to come.

As parents we need to check out our own attitudes to the messages we convey. It is important to become aware of what we say and how we say it, and just what effect this will have upon our children.

The Expression of Inferiority
The behavior that arises out of an underlying inferiority may show itself in one of three ways, such as: defiance, compliance, and withdrawal. The more the parents meet the child's basic need to be loved and understood, the less the child will tend to follow one of these behavior patterns. The less a child feels loved by his parents, the more intensely he will demonstrate one of these patterns.

1. *Defiance.* The defiant child develops this pattern in his earlier years as he learns to bypass his parents'

efforts to control his behavior. He may do this by ignoring
them, wearing them down, throwing fits on the floor, holding his breath until he turns blue, frustrating them so badly
that they give up, or exercising guilt and sympathy control.
He is out to get his own way, and will view any requests on
the parents' part as a violation of his liberties. He will develop a strong resentment toward having to do anything he is
asked to do. When he becomes an adult, he will tend to
resent anyone making any demands on him, will have a
strong need to have his own way, and will have no fear of
aggressively confronting people to get what he wants and
blaming others for his failures.

2. *Compliance.* The compliant child develops his
pattern of life because he is unable to get his own way. He is
afraid of his parents' disapproval and their discipline. He
loses too much of his self-worth under chastisement, and is
therefore willing to compromise in order to reserve his own
sense of worth. Because he doesn't want to be a nobody, he
makes sure he obeys carefully what is asked of him. He feeds
upon the praise that he gets for his obedience and repression
of his inner aggressive impulses. He will tend to behave well,
and views himself as being good. On becoming an adult, he
will tend to be passive, avoid open conflict, and be somewhat
insensitive to his own wishes. He may actually be a hostile
person, but will express his hostility in passive, dependent
ways. He is subject to being overcome by guilt feelings and
depression. He will tend to be pessimistic and negative.

3. *Withdrawal.* The withdrawn child develops his
pattern because he is unable to be either defiant or compliant, as he fears the wrath of his parents very intensely. He
will attempt to avoid feeling dependent on others because to
get close means to get hurt. He will maintain a respectable
distance at all times. He may substitute things and activities
for relationships to people, may be very busy about praise-
worthy things, but avoids socializing on every level. He is
fearful of revealing his own hostile feelings for fear that
others will reject him.[5]

Ways to Build Self-esteem
There are some very basic things that parents can
do to enhance the self-esteem of their child.

1. *Every parent needs to openly demonstrate love and warmth toward his child* from the very beginning. He must frequently tell the child that he loves him and that he is very important to him. The parent also needs to demonstrate affection in tangible ways such as: the pat, touch, hugs, and squeezes. Affection is very meaningful to any child.

2. *The parents should express praise and appreciation to their child.* This should not be limited to jobs that are well done, but it is also important to recognize effort, when the effort is there, even though it isn't exactly right. The child knows when he is trying hard, when you notice it, and when you appreciate it. Be especially supportive when children have not only tried hard, but have done a job well. Tell them such things as, "I'm proud of you." "That was good." "You're really working hard." Don't be afraid of too much praise. Some parents seem to be afraid their kids will become too proud. Actually pride arises not from too much praise, but as an overcompensation for an underlying feeling of inferiority. Don't be flattering or phony. Be realistic in your comments, but look for positive things that you can say to your children.

3. *Take time with your kids.* Take time to read them stories, play games with them, play ball in the backyard, do a puzzle together, and share many other little things that are important to them. These are often the precious times when kids open up concerning important topics. Take them out to the hamburger place of their choice. Go on picnics as a family. Frequently, the simple things you've done with them that don't cost a dime are extremely important to the kids, and are most remembered. Listen to their chatter and to their tales of woe. They need to be heard as much as you do. Take them with you when you're going out on an errand, and let them know that you want their company.

4. *Support them when they're discouraged.* Kids need encouragement as much as anyone. They have frustrating times with homework problems that are hard to understand, problems with other kids, doubts about how to complete a task, and many other difficulties. Help them with their frustrations, and encourage them. Cuts and bruises simply require the miracle working of a Band-Aid and a couple of hugs. If a child seems to be balking at a job that

needs to be done, pitch in and help him get started. You'll be amazed at how fast the job gets done. When children seem to be stuck, encourage them to try again in a new way. Teach them that problems are not to be run away from, but are to be overcome.

5. *Acceptance.* Teach your child that you love him no matter what happens. Avoid the message, "I love you when you do well." A's on a report card are nice, but it's far more important to show that you love your child, rather than whether he gets A's, B's, C's, or D's, as long as he does the very best he can do. Don't qualify your love. Grades are not the most important thing in life; but helping a child find himself and learn how to deal with the various hurdles of life that come his way are of far greater value than a perfect report card. Teach your child that love does not come from material things either. Buy what they need and what is reasonable, but don't be afraid to say, "No." *You can never buy a child's love,* no matter how much you give him. He would far rather have your *time* and your giving of *yourself.*

Teach your child that you love him because he is yours. He'll always belong to you no matter what happens. There will be times of hurt, disappointment, frustration, and discouragement, but you'll always love him and want the best possible for him.

6. *Teach him that God loves him also.* Teach him that God has demonstrated his love in the person of Christ on this earth. He gave his life upon the cross for each of us that our sins might be forgiven and taken away. He, in turn, puts the Spirit of God within us to teach us and to lead us in the right way from day to day. He is with us always; he will never leave or forsake us. God's love is unconditional. He accepts us as we are. Teach your child that God has a long-range plan for his life and is at work helping him develop it even now. Teach your child that he is somebody important to you and to God, and neither you nor God will ever forsake him.[6]

As parents, don't let the pressures of society mold you. Proverbs 31:30 tells us, "Charm is deceptive, and beauty is fleeting; but a woman who fears the Lord is to be praised." In 1 Samuel 16:7 we find the account of the prophet seeking to choose the future king of Israel. We read, "But the Lord said to Samuel, 'Do not consider his appearance or his height, for I have rejected him. The Lord does not look at the things man looks at. Man looks at the outward appearance, but God looks at the heart.' '' We have also an account in Luke 18:18-24, where the rich young ruler came to Jesus looking for the key to eternal life. He had lived a clean, moral life, and had been one of the "good guys." However, he was still greatly influenced by material things and his great wealth. When he learned that he had to shift his loyalty from material things to eternal things of God, he went away sad, because those things were far more important to him than the riches that God offered.

Parents, be careful that you are not forced into the same mold of feeling inferior and second rate because you do not measure up to the requirements of our society in beauty, intelligence, and wealth. Being right with God, belonging to him and feeling important to him, is of far greater value than any of these.[7] Learn this for yourself, and your children will in turn learn it from you.

Workbook Section Chapter Five

1. *Values.*

I have always held these values to be very high. (Check as appropriate.)

_____ beauty	_____	success, getting
_____ intelligence		ahead
_____ material goods	_____	love, affection
_____ obedience	_____	compassion
_____ creativity		for others
_____ honesty	_____	humility
_____ hard work	_____	(others) _____
_____ aggressiveness	_____	_____

Go back over the list, including those you have added. Which are the three most important to you? Number them.

Go over the list again. Which are inspired by society? Mark these with with "S." Which are part of God's system? Mark with a "G."

Where do I need to shift the emphasis in my life?

From _____ to _____ , and from _____ to _____ .

2. *Conflicting messages.*

After thinking about it, I can see that I probably confuse my kids by giving them conflicting messages. Sometimes:

I tell them _____ ,

but then I _____ .

I tell them _____ ,

but then I _____ .

I tell them _____ ,

but then I _____ .

3. Building self-esteem.

Some things I do and say that help build self-esteem in my kids are:

_____   _____
_____   _____
_____   _____
_____   _____
_____   _____
_____

Some things I need to do to help my child feel more worth-while as a person are:

_____   _____
_____   _____
_____   _____

Some things I need to stop doing are:

_____   _____
_____   _____
_____   _____

[1]James Dobson, Hide or Seek (Old Tappan, N.J.: Fleming H. Revell Co., 1974), pp. 22-55.

[2]Silvano Arieti, ed., American Handbook of Psychiatry (New York: Basic Books, Inc., Publishers, 1959), p. 817.

[3]Ibid., p. 65.

[4]Satir, pp. 36, 37.

[5]Wagner, pp. 85-87.

[6]For further study on God's abiding and unchanging love, look up the following passages: John 3:16; 10:27-29; 2 Corinthians 5:21; and Philippians 1:5, 6; and other related Scriptures.

[7]Romans 12:2.

Six

The Problem of Defiance

The father tells his teenage son to be in by 11:00 p.m. The son tartly replies, "I'll do what I want."

A mother tells her adolescent daughter to pick up the things she has left lying around. The daughter replies smartly, "Bug off. Leave me alone."

A mother tells her ten-year-old son not to take his soda or potato chips in the living room. The son replies defiantly, "I'll throw it all over you!"

An adolescent daughter screams at her mother because she has no clean clothes to wear. The mother calmly replies, "But you didn't bring them down to be washed. How was I to know?" The daughter screams back, "You never do anything for me, you lazy _____ _____ . You don't really care!" The mother tries hopelessly to defend herself in this war of words and challenges, finally gives up in defeat from the withering blast, drops everything else, and does an emergency wash to accommodate her "lovely" daughter.

A mother pleads with her young son, "Please, Tommy, pick up your blocks. You know that mother has to get ready for company coming very soon." Tommy goes on playing as if he heard nothing. Mother tries again with the same approach, maybe a little stronger, but no response. After she has told Tommy a dozen times, "This is the last time I'm going to tell you," she realizes that nothing is working. The exasperated mother gives up and picks up the things herself, while Tommy goes off to pull something else out to play with.

While everyone else is quietly praying in church,

Junior is staring at the person behind him and quite audibly remarks, "Hey, you have a tooth missing." The parent tries to turn him around, saying, "Be quiet and I'll give you some candy after church." Junior promptly whacks the kid in front of him on the head with a hymn book. The parent warns, "Look, if you don't settle down, I'm going to have to spank you at home." The child loudly blurts out, "This is boring!" Shaken and thoroughly embarrassed, the parent takes him out, too humiliated to return. Outside, the parent pleads with the child, "Don't you know you're embarrassing me? Why don't you behave yourself?" But nothing changes.

What parent has not gone through the endless stream of excuses or reasons for not going to bed at night, and having the child get up a hundred times after being tucked in bed.

The list is endless. If the parents are defeated, the kids are triumphant. As a result, the kids grow up not respecting the parent's standards, wishes, or attempted controls. Disrespect of parents and defiance of authority have become a national epidemic in our land, where the kids are basically running the parents, and the parents are rushing about trying to forestall the next maneuver. A basic *power struggle* is at stake that *must be faced and conquered as soon as possible.*

Advice
Numerous child raising philosophies have been put out to the general public. Some of these can be summarized as follows:

1. A child will eventually respond to patience, tolerance, and above all, love. No discipline is really required. Just work with the child, and eventually he will come around.

2. Encourage the child to express his anger and rebellious feelings, for there is great value in release of pent-up emotions. This will clear the way for the child to think constructively and practically.

3. The conflict between parents and child is simply a difference of opinions and the parent needs to show his understanding of the child's different view. For example,

"You don't like me because I make you pick up your things."[1]

4. There is a great deal of humanistic teaching today which simply says that a child is born innately good, that any wrong behavior is learned either from his parents or from the society around him. The over-simplification of this is the belief that if a child is left completely to himself, he will do the right things. Any wrong things he learns are, therefore, the automatic responsibility of his parents or the way they brought him up.

5. Cultivation. Another theory is that every child is like a tender bud which must be cultivated in order to bloom. The parent must be careful that he does not destroy the bud by too much handling, but simply cultivate growth by encouragement.

6. There is a strong belief that spanking will encourage violence in children as they grow up. Therefore, the parents should refrain from all spanking and the children will grow up supposedly violence free.

In spite of many studies, philosophies, and ideas, there has nevertheless been a downward trend in the area of respect toward authority. Violence, destruction of property, defiance of authority, and anarchy have become an ever-increasing problem in our society. What is happening to the old concept of "respect for elders"?

Kids are smarter than we think. They are quite adept at learning how to get the results they want for the moment, and can think of five hundred more ways to manipulate the parent to their own ends. This ability seems to flow rather naturally from the child, even one from the best of homes.

The facts point toward the simple truth that a child left to himself does not grow up to do the right and the good, but he becomes selfish, self-centered, self-willed, defiant, irresponsible and undisciplined, lost and aimless. Heredity does not prepare a child to face the responsibilities of life. *Responsible behavior has to be taught, and taught from the time the child is small until it becomes an inner part of his own behavior and value system.* Honesty, truthfulness, unselfishness are values that are taught and demonstrated. These traits are passed on to the child through parents who teach them by example, verbal explanations, and other forms of reinforcement.

How to Overcome Defiance

1. *Distinguish between defiance and immaturity.* It is vital for the parent to know when the child is being defiant, and when the act is simply one of immaturity. For example: to view a two-year-old as defiant because he spills his milk frequently at mealtimes is not realistic. A two-year-old simply does not yet have the coordination to be able to handle a glass of milk adequately and there will be accidents. This is simply immaturity which he will grow out of in due time. Be patient. Think ahead, and don't leave a lot of things in his way to knock over. Better control will come later as the child is encouraged to be careful. He is not being defiant, and severe punishment at this point would only undermine his self-esteem.

The next chapter will deal more specifically with what kind of behavior to expect at different age levels. For example, it is quite natural for a two-year-old to be pulling things out and looking at them simply out of childhood curiosity, with resulting chaos. For a seventeen-year-old to be doing the same is no longer natural. It is rather natural for a nine-year-old to forget to feed his dog from time to time, forget to cut the grass, to take out the trash, and to say please, etc. The same behavior from a seventeen-year-old is no longer acceptable.

Demanding statements from teenagers such as, "Wash my clothes," "Get my dinner," "Don't tell me what to do," "I'm going out whether you like it or not," are all obvious defiance toward parental authority.

There are kids who do precisely what they are told *not* to do, such as: "Don't go outside without your coat." They just ignore requests and commands given, or chronically produce a battle of wits to wear down the parents with maneuvers such as: tantrums, repeated excuses, and ploys of different kinds to get around the parents' will. Playing on the sympathy of the parent, and making the parent feel guilty, are likewise acts of definite defiance. Add also the continual resistant attitude such as: "I don't feel like it," or "Why should I?"

Each of these is an illustration of parents and children locked into combat to determine *who is in charge*. Each brings its share of confusion and grief to the home.

2. *Aim to bend the will, not crush the spirit.* Defiance must be dealt with directly and decisively. However, its long range purpose must be correction through teaching, rather than simply venting one's own hostilities and frustrations on the children. The parent is not out to get revenge. His purpose is to train his children in the way they should go. Bruce Narramore in his book, *Help! I'm a Parent*, gives a helpful description of the difference between discipline and punishment in the following chart.[2]

	PUNISHMENT	DISCIPLINE
Purpose	To inflict penalty for an offense.	To train for correction and maturity.
Focus	Past misdeeds.	Future correct acts.
Attitude	Hostility and frustration on the part of the parent.	Love and concern on the part of the parent.
Resulting emotion in the child	Fear and guilt.	Security.

Any parent is at some time tempted to punish for his own convenience. After a lot of aggravation, the parent may send his kids off to bed early because he's simply tired of all the hassle of trying to get them to do what they're supposed to do. Hence, one kid may remark to the other, "How come when *they* are tired, *we* have to go to bed?" The purpose of discipline is long-range teaching of values to the child. Deal with each instance of defiance *quickly* and *decisively,* and there will not usually be a long list of problems throughout the day.

Neither is defiance on the part of the child an opportunity for a parent to *ventilate* his anger. Many a child's ego has been crushed, his self-confidence destroyed because of overpunishment. He may fall into chronic self-blame because of frequent overreaction on the part of the parent. The goal again is simply to *correct defiant behavior,* but *not to destroy the child.* The parent must struggle to control his own anger in order to obtain this purpose. Hollering and screaming in most cases are usually not the best way to communicate. *Action* will bring far better results than *anger.* A quick swat on the behind, being sent to his room until he can calm down, or for some older children, denial of a desired privilege are good examples. When a child goes beyond the reasonable boundaries set by the parent, he must know that some punishment surely follows. A simple cause and effect relationship needs to be firmly established. The reason for the punishment is not because, "You exasperate me," but because it is vital that the child learn to respect the authority of his parents in order that there be a basic peace and a sense of order in the home.

3. *Insist on Basic Rules.* Reasonable rules are essential to any well-ordered household and to basic security for each member of the family. Most children are well aware of the value of rules and know that without them, chaos follows. What many parents do not seem to understand is that kids actually want some rules to go by. Don't be fooled by their initial resistance, as this has a different meaning. I've had kids tell me personally, "My parents don't love me because they don't make me do what I should do." Kids know very well that they are not able to control their own

limits. They want you to say no when it is appropriate to say no. Even though they may try and connive, they really do not want you to give in. They actually feel more secure and more in control of themselves when you as a parent maintain your authority. They still are selfish at times and want their own way, but children know that they do not have the self-control that is needed to keep themselves on the right track. Therefore, they depend on you as parents to help them. Thus, you should *set reasonable rules for your kids and require that they follow them.*

Make your rules *clear* and *concise.* Spell them out. For example, "On school nights, I want you to turn off the TV and be ready for bed by 9 o'clock. This does not mean 9:15 or 9:30, but 9 o'clock." It is important then that the parent is consistent in requiring that the rule be followed each school night with basically few exceptions.

It is important that the parent also make it clear that any manipulations to get out of basic reasonable requirements will be dealt with firmly either by spanking, loss of privileges, or isolation, whichever works best.

Some examples of manipulative devices children may use are:

>   *Delaying*—Never getting to the task so that the parent eventually does it for him.
>   *Complete ignoring*—Acting like he never heard, in hopes the parent will forget what he is asking.
>   *Whining*—"It's too hard," "I can't help it," seeking pity so the parent will do it himself.
>   *Wearing down*—Persistent questions of "why me, why not later, I don't feel like it," etc., on and on without end, until parent gives up in exasperation.
>   *Forgetting*—When excessive, it is done in hopes that the parent will become frustrated enough to do it himself. Some forgetting is normal, as children are not thinking on the same channels as adults.
>   *Outright resistance*—"I won't do it, try and make

me." A direct challenge to the parent's authority, hoping the parent will back off from his or
her demands.

Tantrums — Yelling and screaming, throwing a
general fit, in hopes the parent will become
sidetracked and back off from his or her demands.

Guilt trips — "You don't love me; my friends aren't
made to do things like this; you're being unfair!" Guilt trips are the ultimate weapon, in-
tended to make the parent feel he is unfit and
back off from his or her demands.

All of these manipulations should be dealt with
firmly by quick and decisive action. Undue attempts at long
explanations, reasons, and concessions only weaken the
needed parental authority and should thus be avoided. Make
it clear what is to be done, and see to it that the mission is
accomplished.

Every parent should understand that kids are basically rule benders. Contrary to popular opinion, the child
is not trying to destroy the parent! He simply wants to see
how far he can go. You can be sure that if you tell him to be in
bed by 9 o'clock without fail, he will try numerous ways to
stay up until 9:15 or 9:30. Precisely at this point, decisive
action must be carried out from the very first test of the
parents' authority. The child will try to bump your rule and
challenge your authority to go as far as he can — to the limit.
Do not bend, do not give in, do not allow yourself to be worn
down. Insist on the reasonable limits already set.

4. Respect for authority. Disrespect for authority
is a serious problem today. Students in school are belligerent
and disrespectful and even abusive toward their teachers.
Some kids go about terrorizing neighborhoods and destroy-
ing property and taunting the local police. Where has all of
this come from?

The first authority figure that the child has to relate to is the authority of his parents. If he is taught respect
for authority in the home, he will carry this respect for other
authority figures in his life, such as: teachers, supervisors,

bosses, civil authorities, etc. If he has learned that respect for authority at home is not required, that he can do and say pretty much what he wants and when he wants without regard for the rights and privileges of others and the authority of his parents, he will carry the same disrespect over to other authority figures as he goes through life. The pattern of defiance toward authority begins at home. With that pattern ingrained within the child, he will find increasing difficulties through life as he tangles with teachers in school, as he loses jobs because of disrespect for bosses, and as he has repeated scrapes with the police. A child such as this is destined to lead a confused life and experience many wasted years — possibly even a life of violence or an early death.

In referring again to Ephesians 6:2, 3, which states, "Honor your father and mother . . . that you may enjoy long life," the direct result of respect and honor toward father and mother is *long life*. Again, clinical experience backs up the teaching of Scripture; for any counselor's case book is full of examples of those who, in defiance of authority, have brought on themselves tremendous amounts of suffering, violence, and even an early death because of their rebellious orientation toward life.

5. *Scriptural teaching on obedience as essential to life*. The Scriptures have a number of things to say about obedience and its vital importance to happiness in life. Proverbs 29:17 says, "Discipline your son, and he will give you rest; he will give delight to your heart" (RSV). Proverbs 19:18 also says, "Discipline your son in his early years while there is hope. If you don't you will ruin his life" (TLB). What statements could be clearer and more to the point than these? Discipline and correct in ways that are appropriate to the child's personality as explained in Chapter Three, but by all means do it while there is time.

6. *Respect for God*. God is the final authority on all matters of faith in life. It is no accident, therefore, that a person who has learned respect and obedience from his parents demonstrates respect and obedience toward God. If a child has learned that disobedience is normal, that disregard for rules and regulations is OK, that belligerence and rebelliousness are acceptable, then the same attitudes carry

throughout his life with other authority figures. The same
dynamics are likewise applied in his personal relationship
toward the final authority, God himself. A person so set in
this direction will bring great trouble on himself, will be in
chronic conflict with others in life, and will be in constant
conflict with his conscience and God as well.

Part of the secret of a long, productive, and happy
life is wrapped up in the learning of obedience, whether it be
obedience to parents, to other authority figures in life, or to
God, who is the Director of life itself. Therefore, it is the
God-given responsibility of every parent to direct his child
in the right way to help him have a happy, productive life.

God himself deals with the whole matter of obedience with his children as well. In 1 Samuel 12:15 we read,
"But if you do not obey the Lord, and if you rebel against his
commands, his hand will be against you, as it was against
your fathers." Just as obedience to parents brings basically a
peaceable homelife, in the same way obedience to God
brings life that is solid and unshakable. Jesus made this clear
in Luke 6:47-49 where he says:

> Everyone who comes to Me and hears My words,
> and acts on them, I will show you whom he is like:
> he is like a man building a house, who dug deep
> and laid a foundation upon a rock; and when a
> flood arose, the river burst against that house and
> could not shake it, because it had been well built.
> But the man who has heard, and has not acted
> accordingly, is like a man who built a house upon
> a ground without any foundation; the river burst
> against it and immediately it collapsed, and the
> ruin of that house was great (NASB).

The conclusion is clear. The learning of obedience
to parents, to other authorities, and to God produces a solid,
peaceful, and long life. The lack of that obedience brings
self-destructiveness to the person. Therefore, as a parent,
teach obedience, act decisively against defiance, and insist
on reasonable respect.

A few words of caution are in order. It is possible
to carry anything too far, no matter how well intentioned.

Many a parent has become locked into mortal battle with a strong-willed child, sometimes needlessly, because of a lack of understanding on the part of the parent. The following are a few important points to keep in mind:

1. *Listen to what the child is saying.* Even if you can't stand the defiance that goes with it, still try to find out what the child is trying to get across. There may be a legitimate need behind all the verbal barrage which needs to be met. Deal with the defiance, but recognize the need and look for some way to meet that need.

2. *Parents are not always right.* You may have miscalculated or misjudged a situation, and the child is defending his or her own rights as a person. Once you suspect that you may be wrong, check into the situation. If you are wrong, *apologize,* and *set the matter straight.* Kids can accept the fact that parents are human and make mistakes better than they can accept the idea that parents are infallible. This is one of the aspects of "not exasperating your children" that Scripture mentions.

3. *Reinforce your teaching with your own example.* By demonstrating how to handle situations, even when you are wrong, you will be giving the needed guidance to the child. Hypocrisy, doing the very thing you tell your child not to do, will provoke a lot of anger within any child. The strong-willed child will be quick to point out the discrepancy, and will respond poorly to the "do as I say, not as I do" philosophy.

4. *Be sure that your rules are reasonable.* Avoid extremes. A long list of rules becomes discouraging. A few clear, simple ones that fit the age and situation of the child will mean far more in the long run than a long involved list. Rules should take into account the child's age and abilities, and likewise his social situation. To ask a two-year-old to wash dishes is courting disaster. To require a teenager to follow rules that completely set him apart from his peer group makes him the "oddball" and subjects him to all sorts of ridicule and rejection from his peer group. This becomes an unbearable pressure to the child which can be the cause of many explosions at home.

5. *Use methods of maintaining order in the home*

that are *appropriate to the situation.* Some children require only a warning "look," others need a verbal warning; some need a spanking, others need to be isolated for a specified period of time; some need withholding of privileges. Don't overdiscipline. Use only enough of whatever works best for your child to keep the order that is necessary to an atmosphere of learning and growing together as a family.

Workbook Section Chapter Six

1. My approach to parenting.
My philosophy of the way to raise children to respect authority has always been: _____
_____
_____
      As far as I can tell, it has been working (circle
one): well, fairly well, poorly, not at all. I could probably
improve this by: _____
_____

2. Rethinking.
      In thinking about my own approach to defiance
and willful disobedience, I find myself (check when appropriate):
_____ being worn down by their manipulations
_____ exasperated to the limit
_____ repeating the same requests over and over
_____ giving up in despair
_____ ventilating my own anger on the child
_____ impulsively changing my requirements, depending
         on how I feel.
_____ losing self-control, hollering, screaming, etc.
_____ hoping for better days to come
_____ standing firm, insisting on obedience
_____ going after the problem before it gets out of hand
_____ punishing defiance
_____ punishing my child for things he does not fully con-
         trol
_____ punishing without really finding out what is going
         on

_____ listening to what my child is saying in spite of his defiant attitude

_____ frequently clashing with my kid in head-to-head combat

_____ trying to be fair

_____ trying to be consistent

_____ trying to be a good example of the same kind of behavior I am asking for

_____ (others) _____

Look over what you have checked. Put an N beside the ones you can see are *not* helpful, that will produce *negative* results. Put a P beside the ones that will produce *positive* results.

> *3. Defiance in my home.*
> Our child shows defiance by:

_____   _____
_____   _____
_____   _____

I find myself responding to that defiance by:

_____   _____
_____   _____
_____   _____

As I think about it, I can see that I need to work further on the problem by giving attention this week to:

_____
_____
_____

Read through the following statements and check whether you agree or disagree.[3]

Agree   Disagree

_____ _____ 1. Children should be required to obey instantly without question.

_____ _____ 2. Parents should give reasons for having certain rules.

_____ _____ 3. Discipline is the same as punishment.

_____ _____ 4. Parents cannot have a clear-cut approach to discipline of their children unless they accept spanking as God's appointed way of discipline.

_____ _____ 5. Children should be allowed to verbalize the bad feelings they have inside of themselves.

_____ _____ 6. Children will learn to take responsibility on their own when they are ready to do so.

_____ _____ 7. Realistically, you cannot reject your child's behavior and still accept the child.

_____ _____ 8. The child should never be allowed to have the last word.

_____ _____ 9. The parent should always stick to what he has said, no matter what.

_____ _____ 10. A loudmouthed kid deserves a good slap in the face.

_____ _____ 11. Kids will eventually grow out of their defiant behavior if you don't pay too much attention to it.

_____ _____ 12. Frequent repetition will wear down the child's resistance and he will eventually obey you.

Discuss your answers with your spouse or a good friend.

[1]James Dobson, *Dare to Discipline* (Wheaton, Ill.: Tyndale House Publishers, 1970), pp. 12, 13.

[2]Bruce Narramore, *Help! I'm a Parent* (Grand Rapids, Mich.: Zondervan Publishing House, 1972), p. 41.

[3]Adapted from Wright, p. 143.

Seven
Distinguishing Immaturity

"My two-year-old child is into everything, throwing out books, writing on walls. He gets all my pots and pans out of the cupboards, and has his toys everywhere. What's wrong? I can't go on like this!"

"My four-year-old child has one cold after another. He wets the bed and has frequent accidents of all kinds. Just yesterday, he fell and knocked out his front teeth. Is my child accident prone? Do I have a hypochondriac? What's wrong with him?"

"My five-and-a-half-year-old child is frequently picking his nose, biting his nails, constantly clearing his throat, and sometimes stuttering. He's driving us all up the wall. Do I have a neurotic child?"

"My thirteen-year-old used to be a very good child, but now she is mouthy, irritable, moody, and sometimes very belligerent. She is constantly on the phone calling her friends that she saw only ten minutes ago. What has happened to my child?"

Actually, there is nothing particularly wrong with any of these children mentioned. Each is going through some basically normal stages of growth and can be expected to show many of these characteristics at different age levels. There are many stages of growth between infancy and adulthood that every parent should understand in order to know what is going on with his or her child.

In 1 Corinthians 13:11 we read, "When I was a child, I talked like a child, I thought like a child, I reasoned like a child. When I became a man, I put childish ways behind me." The implication of the passage is that there are definite steps between infancy, childhood, and adulthood. Each step has various obstacles and hurdles to be overcome in order for the child to reach adulthood. Such tasks as walking, feeding oneself, talking, taking responsibilities, completing school, etc., are a few of these. Even adults find a number of steps of ongoing growth throughout their own lives. After completing school, there are such tasks as preparing for a suitable career, finding and holding a job, finding a spouse, raising a family, working through the many demands on one's time and energy, adjusting to the ever-changing needs of the family, such as the empty nest syndrome, retirement, etc.

Every parent at some time struggles with these questions: "Is my child normal? What can I expect? What will he grow out of? What are warning signs to tell me that he needs special help?"

Many parents are worried that they have a very neurotic child, when actually, he is simply going through some of the fits and starts that every child faces, more commonly called "growing pains." It is important, then, to know what to expect at various ages in order to be assured that your child is not going off the deep end.

Learning Hurdles to Be Crossed
Every child born into this world has many hurdles which he has to overcome in order to reach successful adulthood. It is extremely essential for a child to be able to handle each step successfully. Each new achievement brings new ability to meet the challenges and all that life can bring. The failure in any one step can bring frustration, a sense of failure, a sense of being different from others, and stunted development in that area, which eventually affects the child's personality. The child then begins to have mounting frustrations which undermine his confidence for other tasks and bring to him further emotional problems as time goes on.

The following will give an outline of some of the basic developmental tasks and growth hurdles to be overcome from infancy to adolescence. Adolescent stages will be covered in a later chapter.

1. *Ages one to six—infancy and early childhood.* In this period, the child's main center of attention is his parents. He is learning some of the following adjustments:

> learning to take solid food
> learning to walk
> learning to talk—starting with very short words and working up to sentences
> toilet training—learning self-control
> learning differences between boys and girls and basic modesty
> achieving physiological stability to do such things as walk, run, play without constantly falling flat on his face
> developing the beginnings of reality concepts, how to handle potentially dangerous situations
> learning to relate emotion to others, beginning with parents and siblings and branching out to others
> developing a conscience—distinguishing between right and wrong, mastering impulses
> learning how to love and be loved

There are dangers that can block the reaching of these goals. Such things as neglect, abuse by parents, deprivation of consistent and appropriate love, harsh treatment or any condition interfering with his achievement and feeling of adequacy, are all blockages to normal growth. Blocks in physical development at one point can also affect the ability to reach one's potential in later life, such as: deformed feet, deafness, cerebral palsy, etc. The point is that failure to conquer the various learning hurdles, physically, mentally, and emotionally, will block the child's growth in that area for many years to come, if left unattended.

2. *Ages six to twelve—middle childhood.* During this time, the child's attention branches out to the neighborhood and to school contacts, and he's learning such things as:

> physical skills, such as participating in games and playground activities
> basic skills required of school children, such as reading, writing, and arithmetic

the give and take of social relationships with neighborhood and school, how to share, winning and losing, being accepted and being rejected by others of his peer group

masculine and feminine roles, what the father and mother do in the home and community

developing a value system, a sense of right and wrong, good and bad, what is better and what is best

making some beginning steps toward personal independence, being able to do many more things for himself, such as dress himself, tie his own shoes, feed himself, and do helpful tasks around the home, etc.

Danger at this stage may come in the form of either excessive competition, or the child's own personal limitations which then lead to failure, which in turn leads to resulting feelings of inferiority and poor work habits.

But with encouragement and help from parents, community, school, and church, most children will make it through these adjustments with a reasonable degree of success.

Basic Stages of Development at Different Ages

Every parent wants to know what to expect in the growth and behavior of his or her child at different points along the way. The following descriptions will give a more accurate picture of each child's developing stages, although none should be taken as iron clad. Individual children may vary somewhat in their rate of growth.

1. *Birth to one year.* In infancy, a child is solely dependent on his parents for his needs. He learns to signal for his needs through the medium of crying. It is up to the parent to do the detective work necessary to determine whether the child is lonely, wet, or feeling pain. Very rapid physical, mental, and emotional development is taking place during this time. Within the first few months, the child is beginning to notice the mother, and then significant others, as well as beginning to respond by gooing and gurgling. By four or five months, the child is beginning to sit up and take some solids. By six months, the child is usually reaching out

for what he wants and is able to grasp it in his hands. He becomes very sociable toward others. By ten months, he is extremely sociable with others, smiles, and exhibits much responsiveness. He is able to respond to simple games like "pat-a-cake," waves "bye-bye," can utter simple syllables such as "da-da," and begins to respond to familiar words. He loves an audience and responds with an appropriate show of his "cute" behavior. He has learned to crawl, and is just beginning to walk.

2. *One to two years.* During the first several months the child has been in a basically harmonious relationship with the parents. However, this happy situation gives way to the beginning of a break. He will pull away from the parents to begin the long journey of becoming a separate individual who wants to try out life his own way. This step is a vital part of his growth. At this point, the cute, dependent child starts to venture and try things for himself, at which point no cherished possession is safe. Many parents resent this new display of behavior, not understanding the greater underlying need to explore, to learn, and to develop one's own independence.

By the age of one-and-a-half, the child is darting everywhere and getting into everything possible. He climbs stairs endlessly. He throws toys back out of his crib and then shouts for you to bring them back, only to throw them out again. He may demonstrate outlets for his tension such as banging his head, shaking his bed, or rocking back and forth. He begins to exhibit temper tantrums in which he just sits down and refuses to move. He may do exactly the opposite of what you ask, such as running in the opposite direction when you call him to come. He will enjoy the opposite, and will respond with some "no's" of his own. During this period, he will not be steady on his feet and may lose his balance. He becomes very impatient because he wants everything *now!* He may learn to speak about ten words.

3. *Two to three.* By age two, the child becomes sure of his own balance. He talks with increasing ease. He has learned to wait at least a minute or two, but not a great deal longer. He can begin to identify such things as hunger, being tired, feeling frustrated, and the need for "potty." Dur-

ing this period he may have many demands before sleep. He will constantly be asking for a drink of water, a story, a kiss good-night, and any number of requests. It is during this period that every parent needs to listen for when things are *quiet* rather than noisy, as the child may be busy systematically emptying drawers and cupboards.

By age two-and-a-half some drastic changes seem to be taking place. The child may become very domineering and demanding. This behavior may range from insisting that he make decisions about things, to becoming very impatient and inflexible about what he gets and how he gets it. It will have to be his way, or no way. At this point he is not adaptable to others in his life and what they expect from him. He may show violent emotion. He may show opposite extremes of behavior in which he's an angel one minute and a devil the next; or he may say, "I love you" very sweetly one minute, and "I hate you" with equal feeling the next. He may walk up to a perfect stranger and kick him or sock him. He may become destructive by tearing the wallpaper off the wall, by shouting and screaming in temper tantrums, or expressing other destructive forms of behavior. This stage, sometimes called the "terrible twos," requires a great deal of patience in the parents. Sometimes it is helpful to divert the child's attention from his area of frustration to something else. Other times just giving the child time to work through his frustration is useful. It should be understood that this is the peak age of unsteady equilibrium in which the child is very unsure of himself and what he is doing. Consequently, he has a lot of frustration in everything that he tries to do.

4. *Three to four.* At first, the child at age three usually experiences a relatively quiet period in direct contrast to the terrible twos. He goes from extreme resistance to one of conformity in which his favorite answer of "No" is replaced by a very pleasant "Yes." He is no longer taking everything he can get from everybody, but he is beginning to learn to share with others. He can now do things your way instead of simply his own. People are becoming more important to him, and he is learning to make friends with others. He listens carefully to adults. He looks for clues of their approval or disapproval. He responds with vigor. He speaks

with animation. This is a time when he has much better coordination and is able to handle daily routines, such as dressing and play activities, rather easily. He actually puts toys away! He begins to make rough drawings on paper.

The frustration and rage of two-and-a-half is just not there. At this point he may be controlled simply by being told what to do. He may be able to feed himself without spilling something at every meal. He may be found riding his tricycle by the hour and in general staying out of trouble. He may tend to overexert himself and fatigue may become a problem.

By age three-and-a-half, we find another abrupt change in which the child seems to be entering a stage of integrating new tasks. He now shows marked insecurity and a lack of coordination. He may stumble, fall easily, and be afraid of heights. During this period he may develop nervous habits such as eye blinking, biting the nails, picking the nose, facial tics, thumbsucking, spitting at others, etc. He will show whining type of behavior, excessive questions, extra sensitivity to how others view him. And he will say such things as, "Don't look at me. Don't laugh at me." He will show a lot of jealousy from attention given to others and will seem to require exclusive attention. It is during this period that the parents will need to exhibit a lot of patience and understanding.

5. *Four to five.* The first part of age four seems to be a continuation of three-and-a-half in which the child just breaks loose in every direction he is not supposed to go. He is just plain out of bounds. He may hit kids, throw stones, bite people, and run away. He may show a lot of silly laughter, fits of rage, and seem to have a sudden vocabulary of "bathroom words." He will show defiance to direct commands and will seem to enjoy being defiant and tough. He may have a lot of tall tales and a very strong imagination about things that he believes happened. He may seem overly confident and brash. He may have many illnesses, frequent colds, stomach-aches, and accidents. However, he is developing some increasing independence, can do limited errands with a parent, and needs to be allowed to try new things as appropriate. Again, the parents will have to be understand-

ing of what is happening as the child is reaching out to do things, but feeling very unsure of himself in the process. The parents should be ready to tighten the reigns when this is necessary and to pull him back as needed.

During the second half of age four, the child is pulling back from his out-of-bounds behavior. He is starting to sort out the difference between real and make-believe. At this age, he can have long discussions about things and be very inquisitive. He may like to draw for long periods and will show rapid growth in intelligence. He will like to hear the same stories over and over again.

6. *Five to six.* Age five becomes basically a delightful time for parent and child alike. The child is reliable, stable, well-adjusted, and seems to feel secure. The child is calm, friendly, and not overly demanding. A child seems basically content with the present situation, and is able to adapt to it. He does not branch out that much during this period. Generally, good health prevails. The child invites and accepts supervision and affection from the parents and seems to thrive on praise for conformity. He likes to help his parents with projects, and asks intelligent questions that deserve straightforward answers. He prefers to play with other kids in group activities. He enjoys cutting, pasting, and drawing. He gains reading readiness. This is an age every parent dreams of. The pot of gold at the end of the rainbow is finally in sight!

7. *Six to seven.* By now the parent has no doubt guessed that it couldn't last. Age six shows the breakup of the equilibrium and a whole new effort of reaching out toward new things begins. Life becomes generally restless. The child becomes very difficult to deal with, much like he was in the "terrible twos." He becomes violent and emotional, and shows opposite extremes. He can say in one breath, "I love you," and in another, "I hate you." The child becomes the center of his world again and will blame his mother for everything that doesn't go the way he wants it to. He wants everything there is to have, and has to win at everything he does. He is rigid in that he has to have his own way, and tears and tantrums will follow when he doesn't get it. This again is a clumsy age and he will frequently be on the brink of disas-

ter. There will again be frequent illnesses, and there will be toilet accidents from overexcitement. There is an initial, "No, I won't" to every demand until it becomes his own idea, at which point he will carry it out. He will become negative, rude, saucy, and argumentative. He will appear to be able to face any new situation head-on with overconfidence and be ready to fight whenever necessary. His vocabulary is increasing rapidly, as is his ability to carry on long conversations with imaginary people. He knows his own address and his parents' names. He knows something about the value of different coins and simple numbers. He is greatly delighted by his beginning steps to learn to read. His attention span is short and he finds it difficult to sit still for long periods.

8. *Seven to eight.* Age seven is a time of withdrawing from combat. The child may complain, may retreat rather than demand, may become sullen, gloomy, mopey, and moody. The child likes to be alone and do things by himself. He may go beyond his physical limits and experience fatigue. The child feels picked on, feels that nobody loves him, and may pout a lot. During this period he gets off the track easily and forgets things he was supposed to do, even though he may have started out quite willingly. He can grasp the basic ideas of addition and subtraction, can tell time, is able to run errands, make purchases, and take responsibility in an increasing amount from this time on. His attention span is still short.

9. *Eight to nine.* During this age the child is out again to meet the world. Everything new and difficult is a challenge to him. He is constantly busy, enjoys any new experience, is trying out new things, and is making new friends. He is aware of many failures, and these bother him. He may complain, "I never get anything right." During this age he wants a good two-way relationship with others and will show give and take. He wants close understanding in the relationship, and will get upset when he feels he is not understood. Accidents are frequent during this period. He is obedient, if you insist, but he may need many tangible rewards, such as money, in order to do things willingly. He may cry when overly fatigued. He can make change for small amounts. He can read the comics. He may show a sense of

humor. He can tell the day, the month, and the year. He becomes interested in the world of faroff places, as well as the distant past. His attention span is increasing.

10. *Nine to ten.* This is a quieter time during a child's life, and he is more within himself. He may become very independent and may resist too much bossing. If the parent can respect this need for independence, he will tend to get along very well. He will show increasing interest in friends outside the family. This will be an age in which he is perfecting his skills. He will tend to worry and take things overly hard, sometimes even going to pieces. This is sometimes called "a neurotic age" in which he has numerous complaints of all kinds, particularly when there is some task that he does not like to perform. He will show numerous physical ailments, usually none of which are serious. With authority figures, he may sometimes either withdraw or rebel. Sometimes he may just simply tune out what the parent is saying. Sometimes he will simply complain, and sometimes he will just "forget." The child is responsive to praise at this point, and positive reinforcement can be used quite effectively.

Intellectually, he is grasping the easier multiplication and division facts. His interest in fantasy declines, and his interest in how things are made increases. His interest in a special area may begin to crowd out some other play activities. Boys' and girls' reading interests become noticeably different at this age.

11. *Ten to eleven.* Sometimes age ten can be a very nice age for the parent to enjoy. The child tends to obey easily and naturally, particularly when there is some gain in his status by obedience. He seems pleased with life, seems satisfied with his parents and his teachers in school. He seems to be able to enjoy himself easily and is friendly toward others around him. He is straightforward, matter-of-fact, flexible, and doesn't take things overly seriously. Every parent should get his fill of this age because the parent *will never again get the same total acceptance from the child!*

For others, this age is the beginning of the adolescent period which can be stormy and tumultuous. The parents may believe that a timebomb has gone off in this formerly quiet, cooperative child. The child becomes defiant, extremely moody, unpredictable, undependable, and in general, a real mess! Early adolescence will be further discussed in Chapter Ten.

Intellectually, the child exhibits some ability to plan ahead and gather factual information. He becomes interested in other people's ideas, and steadily grows in his capacity for thought and reasoning, which makes creative companionship with parents more desirable than ever. He is able to use numbers beyond 100 and to handle simple fractions.

The Overall Pattern

The observant reader will notice that there seems to be an alternating pattern between fits and starts as the child begins to expand into new stages. This is followed by a time of relative calm in which the child seems to be integrating his previous experiences. The fits and starts predominate for a time, then gradually give way to a period of calm and catching up with one's self.

In their book entitled, *Child Behavior,* authors Ilg and Ames give a schematic representation of the repeating pattern of the calm periods, with the fits and starts of expanding behavior that follows.[1]

Child's Age			Characteristic Behavior
2	5	10	smooth, consolidated
2½	5½-6	11	breaking up
3	6½	12	rounded, balanced
3½	7	13	turned inward
4	8	14	vigorous, expansive
4½	9	15	inward-outward, troubled, neurotic
5	10	16	smooth, consolidated

It is important for each of us as parents to recognize these various stages, and to deal with them accordingly. Even though a child is at a violent stage, this may be perfectly normal behavior for that age. However, the parent must provide limits by curbing and controlling behavior, together with the demonstration of love. The child is struggling to get hold of new things, but unable to keep his own self-control properly at that point. He needs some guidance from his parents to know what are appropriate limits for his behavior, which in turn helps him to integrate these within himself before his next developmental step. The knowledge of what to expect at different ages also helps each of us as parents to have some basic peace of mind. It helps to know that fits of temper at a certain age don't mean that the child has gone berserk, or that you as a parent have badly goofed. The kid just may be normal after all!

It should be understood that these are only guidelines, and that children do in fact develop at somewhat different rates. But any far-reaching differences may indicate some developmental immaturity or irregularity that merits some further evaluation, or possibly professional consultation.

Parallels to Christian Growth

There are many parallels between child development and growth in the Christian life. There are numerous passages in Scripture that indicate that our life is basically a long period of growth with many fits and starts along the way. Our beginning is illustrated by 1 Peter 2:2 which says, "Like newborn babies, crave pure spiritual milk, so that by it you may grow up in your salvation, now that you have tasted that the Lord is good." This tells us that we start out in the Christian life just as a baby starts out in life, feeding on the simplest food of all. We cannot take more solid foods until we have reached the correct step in our growth. In 1 Corinthians 3:2, Paul writes, "I gave you milk, not solid food, for you were not yet ready for it. Indeed, you are still not ready." This indicates that first and early steps of Christian growth have to be reached before the children of God are ready for other steps.

Some of the more specific learning hurdles in the Christian growth are indicated by passages such as James 1:2-4:

> Consider it pure joy, my brothers, whenever you
> face trials of many kinds, because you know that

> the testing of your faith develops perseverance.
> Perseverance must finish its work so that you may
> be mature and complete, not lacking anything.

The point of the text is simply that we cannot jump from the
beginning to the end without some intermediate steps. We
must go through some periods of testing of our faith in order
to develop the ability to endure.

Before we can reach maturity, our endurance must
be tested and strengthened. In 2 Peter 1:4-8 we find a rather
similar idea:

> Through these he has given us his very great and
> precious promises, so that through them you may
> participate in the divine nature and escape the
> corruption in the world caused by evil desires. For
> this very reason, make every effort to add to your
> faith goodness; and to goodness, knowledge; and
> to knowledge, self-control; and to self-control,
> perseverance; and to perseverance, godliness; and
> to godliness, brotherly kindness; and to brotherly
> kindness, love.

Here are a series of growth steps that must be obtained in
order to reach maturity. The first starts out with faith, which
then must move on to the development of goodness. Goodness must develop knowledge. After knowledge comes a
step of self-control. After self-control comes the step of perseverance, after which follows godliness, after which follows the step for brotherly kindness, and the final step of a
deeper love, which is patterned after God's love itself.

The simple point is that there are definite steps
that must take place in the Christian life. None of these may
be bypassed or we get stuck at that point. There must be
development in one area in order for development to follow
in the next. The same principles apply in both the physical
and spiritual realms for us as parents. Then we apply them to
our children in their physical, emotional, intellectual, and
spiritual growth in preparing them for life.

Workbook Section Chapter Seven

1. *Family stages.*

In applying this information to my own family, I can expect the following behavior from each of my kids as follows:

Name _____ Age _____

Expected behavior: _____

_____

_____

_____

Name _____ Age _____

Expected behavior: _____

_____

_____

_____

Name _____ Age _____

Expected behavior: _____

_____

_____

_____

2. *The results.*

My kid(s) (fit, don't fit, partially fit) most of the characteristics for their own age level. This means that I should (check one):

_____ thank God for small blessings

_____ give it up as a lost cause

_____ panic, rush him off to a professional

_____ think through his general pattern of development*
_____ look for ways to strengthen specific areas of weakness
_____ all of the above

*For example, the child may be slow in achieving most of his growth milestones, and will therefore probably be slow in others; or the child may develop quickly intellectually, but slower socially, or vice versa.

3. Adjustments.

I realize I may have been expecting too much for the present age of my child by _____ and need to adjust my own approach by _____.

4. Share experiences.

Talk with someone else nearby (spouse, friend, or someone studying this material along with you) about your experiences with your child at different stages, and ask them to share their experiences with you. There is a lot we can learn from each other.

[1]Frances L. Ilg and Louise Bates Ames, *Child Behavior* (New York: Perennial Library, Harper and Row Publishers, 1955), p. 12.

Eight
Tools for Developing Maturity

A child has just blazed a trail from the front door to his bedroom to the bathroom and out the back door. The path consists of jackets, books, clothes, and bubble gum wrappers. You had just cleaned up the house and are about to scream.

You get a storm of protest and grumbling any time you ask for a simple favor from your child. "Why can't they just do what they're asked?" you say.

Your child's constant whining and complaining is driving you crazy. Is there anything you can do?

You have to tell Junior the same things over and over and over again, but get no response until finally you really get tough. Is there anything that you can do about this?

Your daughter finally completed her school assignment after long hours of hassle, cajoling, and persuasion. But she carried it around in her notebook for a week, never handing it in. She gets a big fat zero as a result.

Your kids have terrible table manners. Evening meals are more like a gathering of pigs at the garbage trough. Is there anything you can do about this?

You can hardly get your kid out of the door for school. A terrible battle takes place every morning; she is always late and you sink in total exhaustion after you finally shove her out the door. Is there anything you can do about this?

Junior continually leaves his bicycle out at night even though you told him again and again that it might be stolen. None of this makes any difference to him. Is there anything you can do about this?

Dealing with Immaturity

Each of the examples above are illustrations of immaturity in a child, something you need to help him or her grow out of. Immaturity is very different from defiance. *Defiance is a direct act of the will in opposition to the parents' will,* a struggle for control. *Immaturity has to do with learning responsibility, behavior, and skills to be developed* that require time and effort.

Simply telling and reminding may work, but many times it does not. There are reasons for this. Kids think in very *short-range terms.* Planning ahead and responsibility are just not part of their thinking pattern. Kid's *priorities* are different. Things like clubhouses, fishing in the pond, swimming in the lake, skating parties, slumber parties, submarines, and *Star Wars* are far more important in the thinking of the child than picking up after himself. Mundane things such as making the bed, picking up papers, and putting things away are definitely not on the "important things to do" list of a growing child. In order to accomplish the task of developing this kind of responsibility, children will need aids to help learning these behaviors.

Law of Reinforcement

There is a specific principle in human behavior which goes something like this: *Behavior which achieves desirable results will recur.*[1] To say it another way, if you like the result when you try something a different way, you are likely to do it that way again.

There are many examples of this principle. The boss says, "I like your style, Jones. Keep up the good work. You'll find something extra in your pay envelope." As a result, Jones is very happy, and he rushes home at the end of the day to tell his wife. But even more important, he has greater incentive to work harder with increased dedication to his job.

A husband says to his wife, "That was a wonderful meal, honey." The wife who tried hard to make it just right glows within, and has increased incentive to make it happen again and try even greater things.

Mother says to her son, "That was a good job, Joey." She gives him a reassuring hug. Joey is pleased that his efforts have been recognized and will try again to do something that will please Mother.

Father sees his young son trying valiantly to push the stubborn lawnmower on a hot day to help his dad. After a long struggle, the father says to the boy, "You've really tried hard. Here's money for ice cream." The boy happily walks away with the money, knowing that his efforts have been noticed, appreciated, and rewarded. He will undoubtedly try to help his father again. His motivation to try is greatly increased.

The opposite principle is also true. As Dobson points out, *behavior that is not reinforced will soon fade away.*[2] When there is no recognition, only constant badgering, enthusiasm drags. When life is all demands and work, with no recognition of any kind, low productivity results. There is little motivation to do things expected when there is no tangible reward. Thus, a person on a job who receives only criticism, but no recognition, for his efforts can get very discouraged. He will have little desire to do the best he can or to improve his performance, but will do enough to just get by.

Using Reinforcement to Develop Responsible Behavior

As parents, we can use the principles of reinforcement to help develop mature behavior in our kids. A few important facts should be clearly understood.

1. *Expectations must be clear and consistent.* Simply telling a child to try harder or do better is unclear and vague. The child does not know what "try harder" means exactly and will either eventually give up and forget out of frustration, or will live in a constant state of tension and anxiety, trying very hard to please the parent, but never really being sure where he stands.

The following are some examples of clear and specific expectations for your child to meet:

I made my bed this morning before I went out.
I said please and thank you at the dinner table.
I completed and handed in all of my homework.
I did what I was told without fussing.
I did not whine today.
I went off to school willingly.
I put my things away before I went to bed.

Each of these is clear and specific and easily understood by a youngster. Explain clearly to the child which of these are to happen on a day-by-day basis or on school days. The parents must then see that they happen on a day-to-day basis, not a day or two here and there.

2. *Short-term thinking.* Deal with only one day at a time. Time moves slowly for children and a reward promised next month seems more like next year. It is useless to tell the child that if he is good you will take him on a camping trip this summer. That is like three years from now to the child. Two weeks of punishment for the wrong kind of behavior is more like six months in solitary confinement to a child whose concept of time is quite different from yours. After a while he forgets why he is being punished and becomes rebellious to the punishment itself.

Deal with one day at a time. Give a review at the end of the day to show the child where he did well and how he needs to improve.

A *behavior chart* can be very helpful in keeping expected behaviors before a child. This way it is easy for him to see what he needs to do and the appropriate check mark or star for the day helps him to see what he has done well and where he needs improvement.

At the end of the week, a positive reward must be given in some form. This will vary with each child as to what is important to him or her. Some will respond to motivation by money; others will want a certain desired privilege, such as bowling, skating, or watching a favorite TV program. Rewards can also be verbal, such as, "That was a good job," or they can be in the form of affection in the sign of a hug.

If a larger item, such as a new bicycle, is being used for motivation, it is advisable to have a tangible visual aid, such as a thermometer chart with a picture of the bicycle at the top. At the end of each week, the child can color in up to the level he has reached toward the goal. The chart provides a visual aid to keep the goal in the child's mind.

3. *Specific rewards.* Each child needs a clear understanding as to what he will receive as a direct result of his efforts. If the reward is rather vague, then the motivation lags, particularly if something goes wrong with that vague promise. The promise, "We might go away somewhere," is quite inadequate. The child needs something tangible that means something to him, a specific place and a specific activity.

The choosing of the reward is very important. Be sure to enlist the child's help in choosing something appropriate. Without his direct interest, motivation will lag, and the goal will be ignored. The goal must be short term and reachable. Putting away money for a car someday has no meaning to a ten-year-old, and not that much even to a teenager. Rewards such as: money, a new bat and ball, new clothes or accessories for a doll, various pieces of fishing tackle, a visit to MacDonald's for hamburgers, a family outing, an extra hour for a TV special, bowling, a skating party, spending the night with a friend, etc., all may well be reachable and desired goals. By using a behavior chart, you can reward the child a nickel a day for each behavior successfully completed. This is a short-term reward a child easily understands. A privilege such as skating may be earned by reaching twenty points for the week. Specific rewards are limited only by the imagination of parent and child working together. State clearly how the reward is to be earned, then follow it through consistently on a daily basis so as to keep the child in touch with the desired behavior as he sees a definite reward for his efforts.

4. *The question of bribery.* Some will immediately object and say that the preceding suggestions are bribery to get a child to do something that he really ought to learn how to do himself. Actually this is not the main issue. Our whole society is built on reinforcement.[3] The working man expects to receive a paycheck as his material reward for his efforts. If his paycheck ceased, but the work requirements

continued, he would soon have little motivation to keep on working. Trophies and recognition are offered for winners in contests and competitive sports. If there was nothing to look forward to, the athlete would not expend all that amount of effort. Medals for bravery are offered to those in the Armed Services as a reward for unusual service. Plaques are given to successful businessmen. Generally honors are given for special achievement. Yet none of us thinks of these as bribery. Rather, we view bribery as illegal or inappropriate action, not the building of responsibility as we are doing with our children.

The building of *motivation* is the main factor. Experience shows, in using a reward system with children, that once a specific area of immaturity has been overcome, the child usually does not need such things as a behavior chart and rewards to help him further with that problem. He is ready to move on to another new accomplishment. The child senses his reaching of this particular accomplishment and this in itself becomes a reward to him. He is now ready to move on to another challenge. Thus the behavior chart may focus on a few particular behaviors to start with, but once some of these are conquered, others may be substituted to help the child to continue in his growth pattern.

5. *Shifting the focus to positive achievement.* One of the first words that each of our children learns is, "No, no!" As parents, we tend to put more emphasis on what is wrong than what is right.

The American Institute of Family Relations reported on a study they had conducted. They asked mothers to keep track of how many times they made negative statements to their children as compared with positive statements. The survey revealed that they criticized ten times for every one time they said something favorable![4]

A particularly spirited child with the inborn ability to get into everything at once provides a number of opportunities for the parent to point out what is wrong. He soon catches on to the idea that he gets more attention for doing wrong than he does for right behavior. Since it is better to be hollered at than to be ignored, he continues on the same track. Thus parents can unintentionally get locked in hand-to-hand combat with the child and actually be encouraging further misbehavior without realizing it. Parents need to think a lot more about what they can do to encourage the right kind of behavior. Try to get away from the focus on what is wrong to focusing on what is right, and build on that. When you do see the right kind of behavior, find tangible ways to express appreciation, to show caring, and to reward the good behavior.

The second basic principle of human behavior, as stated earlier, tells us that if wrong behavior is ignored long enough it will eventually go away. A good application of this principle would be in the treatment of childish tantrums. If a parent tries to talk the child out of his tantrum, tries to somehow persuade him to calm down when he's in the midst of one, the tantrums will continue on and on. However, if the parent totally ignores the tantrum and walks away from it, leaving no audience, the child will soon give up that manipulative device. It has no reward any longer. It is better if the parent waits for the child to make an effort to do something and then tells him, "I like it when you try to make the best of a situation and fit in with the family instead of throwing a fit about every little thing." Then the child is more likely to try to fit into the family, rather than throwing the tantrum to get his own way. Again the parent must clearly identify the wrong behavior and purposely ignore it no matter how hard the child tries to get attention. Isolate the child if necessary. Send him to his room until he calms down. That way he gets no attention and eventually is more willing to try a better way.

There must be a balance of *ignoring the wrong kind* of behavior and *rewarding the right kind.*

Worthy of mention also is the fact that a parent does not need to recognize the child *every* time he does something right. That would become unnaturally repetitious after a while. Actually, better results are achieved when the parent recognizes and encourages the right behavior from time to time, which in turn reassures the child that he is on the right track, and that this is appreciated by his parents.

6. *A sample behavior chart.* Page 119 shows an example of a behavior chart which could be suitable for

younger children ages four to six.[5] It can be easily modified to fit other age levels. Fill in the chart daily, and add the totals for the day. As the child gets older, the chart may be modified to suit his particular needs. The totals may then go for the week and the appropriate rewards be given.

7. *Positive reinforcement for teenagers.* Teenagers are a somewhat different breed. However, many of the same principles are also workable for them in a modified form. The following principles will be helpful:

a. *Decide what to use for incentives.*

Things like use of the family car for a few hours can be a very powerful incentive. Also, teenagers are always in need of clothes to help them fit in and meet the latest pressure from their peer group. So extra money for dates and other activities can be very helpful.

b. *Formalize an agreement.*

Work out a specific agreement (contract) with a teenager to do certain chores in which they may earn certain points to gain a desired privilege.[6] Examples:

wash the car weekly	25 pts.
mow the lawn, yardwork, housework	30 pts./hr.
baby-sitting	15 pts./hr.
room straightened daily	5 pts.
each hour of study	15 pts.

At the end of the week the points are added up, and once a goal is reached of, say 1,000 pts., the privilege may be granted. There are also to be penalties for unreasonable behavior which may set him back if he has been very mouthy and defiant or very uncooperative. Many times a written contract in which the teenager agrees to do certain things in return for certain rewards can be very useful.

c. *Establish a system of immediate rewards.*

If a teenager earns a reward, even if you have doubts and fears about it, then by all means you must give it, as this is the agreement. If he does not earn it, then by all means, do not give it to him. He has lost out and must accept the responsibility for his own lack of effort with no excuses.[7]

We have thus discussed the principles of positive reinforcement and its value in learning the skills of responsible behavior. The tools have been given and may be used as presented or modified to fit the situation. The basic principles still remain.

8. *Long-range results.* With the proper use of motivation as outlined, some very important long-range results can be accomplished. The repeated use of these principles helps to develop a number of important characteristics in the child that are useful for years to come. Some of these characteristics are as follows:

> ability to learn new skills
> ability to face a task and follow it through to completion
> dependability
> ability to handle routine responsibilities as a natural part of life
> confidence that he can do things, and the willingness to systematically work at something until it is conquered
> inner pride of accomplishment
> freedom to take on even greater challenges

In addition, there are a number of long-range rewards. The child who has carried these characteristics over into adult life, because he has been helped to learn them in childhood, will experience some of the following rewards for his efforts:

> praise and recognition from others for his abilities
> self-enhancement—job promotions, personal satisfaction
> knowledge of how to inspire growth in his children
> knowledge of how to motivate significant others, such as employees, friends, fellow workers, which in turn brings more recognition and praise

"MY JOBS"

November 14 15 16 17 18 19 20 21 22 23 24 25 26 27

	14	15	16	17	18	19	20	21	22	23	24	25	26	27
1. I brushed my teeth without being told														
2. I straightened my room before bedtime														
3. I picked up my clothes without being told														
4. I fed the fish without being told														
5. I emptied the trash without being told														
6. I minded Mommy today														
7. I minded Daddy today														
8. I said my prayers tonight														
9. I was kind to little brother Billy today														
10. I took my vitamin pill														
11. I said "thank you" and "please" today														
12. I went to bed last night without complaining														
13. I gave clean water to the dog today														
14. I washed my hands and came to the table when called														
TOTAL														

Scriptural Examples of Positive Reinforcement

There are numerous examples from Scripture whereby positive Christlike behavior is tangibly rewarded. It will not be possible to mention all of these, but a few are noted to help establish this as a clear principle of life.

1. *Psalm 1* talks about the man who resists the council of the wicked and refuses to join the way of sinful men. It describes his reward as *happiness* and *delight* as he follows in the Word of God, and describes him as a person who is *prosperous* and *fruitful in life*. These are tangible rewards received for following godly behavior.

2. *Matthew 10:42.* Jesus simply stated that, "If anyone gives a cup of cold water to one of these little ones because he is my disciple, I tell you in truth, he will certainly not lose his *reward.*" A simple act of kindness toward others in the name of Christ has *positive rewards*.

3. *Ephesians 6:5-8.* The servant is told to "serve wholeheartedly, as if you were serving the Lord, not men, because you know that the Lord will reward everyone for whatever good he does, whether he is slave or free." The motivation of the Christian is different from that of a non-Christian, as a child of God is seeking to work as though he were working for God himself. He receives a *higher reward* which encourages him and motivates him to continue on.

4. *Matthew 5:10-12.* In the Sermon on the Mount, Christ said,

> Blessed are those who are persecuted because of righteousness, for theirs is the kingdom of heaven. Blessed are you when people insult you, persecute you and falsely say all kinds of evil against you because of me. Rejoice and be glad, because great is your reward in heaven, for in the same way they persecuted the prophets who were before you.

Here is motivation for endurance in the midst of suffering and ridicule for the sake of Christ. There is *reward* promised at the end which *spurs* us forward toward the *desirable behavior*.

5. *James 1:12* says, "Blessed is the man who perseveres under trial, because when he has stood the test, he

will receive the crown of Life that God has promised to those who love him." Here again is *motivation* for perseverance when a difficulty is given, the motivation being the *reward* of the *Crown of Life* for those who love God.

6. *John 15:5-7.* Christ talks about the necessity of abiding in the Vine, or to say it another way, to draw one's strength from him. The *reward* of abiding in him is the *bearing of much fruit,* and also *answered prayer.* The absence of abiding in Christ produces a life of nothingness.

Not only do we see the principles of positive reinforcement in teaching responsible behavior and fostering maturity in our children, we see it in every walk of life, and we see it as a sound principle of the Christian life. As parents, then, let us not hesitate to put this principle to good use in raising our children.

Workbook Section Chapter Eight

1. *Behavioral problems.*
Jot down several behavioral problems in your child that you see he needs to develop in order to grow up. Try to keep them appropriate to his age level.

_____	_____
_____	_____
_____	_____
_____	_____

Take the five that you see are the most important ones (for younger children). Put a check beside these.
Restate each of these in very clear and specific terms that your child can understand.

_____	_____
_____	_____
_____	_____
_____	_____

2. *Rewards.*
Think about what kind of short term reward your child might be interested in, such as money, other material rewards, or a privilege. List a few of these; discuss it with your spouse, and check it out with your child.

_____	_____
_____	_____

3. *Behavior motivation system.*
Put together a behavior motivation system tailored for your child. This may be in the form of a chart for your younger kids, with duties listed, marked daily, and totals tallied at least weekly. For teens it may take the form of a contract which may include points earned for each task

completed and a final agreed-upon reward once a specified total of points is reached. You may use the blank samples on the next pages, or make your own.

Put it to use on a consistent daily basis. Make changes where necessary to further improve the plan. Once a specific behavior is conquered, replace it with another that needs attention.

4. *Verbal reinforcement.*

Think of some things your child does that are worthy of some verbal reinforcement or other tangible rewards. List a few.

Positive behavior   Tangible reinforcement

_____   _____

_____   _____

_____   _____

Sample Chart: Younger Child

MY JOBS	M	Tu	W	Th	F	Sat	Sun	Totals
1.								
2.								
3.								
4.								
5.								

Total for week _____

Sample Chart: Teens

Duties	Points Earned
1.	
2.	
3.	

4. _____ | _____
5. _____ | _____
6. _____ | _____

Total _____

When _____ points are earned, you will receive _____

_____ .

Signed (parents) _____

(teen) _____

Date: _____

[1]Dobson, *Discipline*, p. 64.

[2]*Ibid.*, p. 78.

[3]*Ibid.*, p. 71.

[4]J. Allen Petersen (ed.), *The Marriage Affair* (Wheaton, Ill.: Tyndale House Publishers, 1973), p. 160.

[5]Dobson, *Discipline*, p. 69.

[6]A contract is a mutual agreement which may be verbal or may be written and signed by both parents to further formalize it.

[7]Dobson, *Discipline*, pp. 91-93.

Nine
Special Problems

"My child is different. He seems slower than others. He seems to be the last one to catch on. He tries very hard, but he never quite catches up."

"My child is bright, yet he seems to lag behind others."

"My child has potential to do the work, but he just don't seem to be that interested. He won't try that hard and is right now in danger of failing."

"My child is like a whirlwind; he is into everything. He has a short attention span, throws tantrums over any little thing, breaks everything he plays with, bites and scratches other kids, is constantly in motion, changes his emotions very quickly, and is a chronic behavior problem in school. I get called every day about him."

"My kid is very spirited and self-willed. You tell him one thing he isn't allowed to do and you can be sure that's just what he will try, unless I really stand over him."

Each of the above descriptions of children's behavior described by their parents represents a particular type of special problem that needs a different approach. With some, a new approach will be helpful; with some, special cooperation between parents and school will be needed; others will need professional help to assist the parents and child together to shape goals for behavior and the steps to reach those goals.

Anything that is troubling a child can definitely affect his school behavior and lead to school failure. Not all school failure is an academic ability problem by any means.

Worries and troubles of various kinds can distract a child from attention to classroom duties. He can be very wrapped up in coping with his new overriding problem and be quite unable to keep his mind on his work.

Some special problem areas along with some suggested approaches to a solution will be presented in the pages that follow.

The Late Bloomer

The late bloomer is a child who is simply somewhat behind in his development.[1] In comparison with other kids, his language may seem somewhat childish. He will have problems with his physical coordination, and will tend to cry easily and appear to be a mama's boy. Because he is naive and somewhat babyish, other kids will take advantage of him. He is not physically ill, nor is he mentally retarded. His development rate is just a bit behind others. As a result of this, he will have difficulty keeping up in school because he'll be immature and just not ready. If he begins his school career at his chronological age, he may well find himself getting further and further behind as time goes on. In spite of his efforts, he will still doodle, look out the window, and appear quite disinterested in class.

It is easy to assume that this child is stupid. He will quickly gain the name of "dummy" from his peers because he will do poorly in academic contests and sports events due to his poor coordination. Humiliation naturally follows, and the frequent sense of failure as well as the destructive teasing from others will eat away at his self-concept. He will begin to feel ignorant, stupid, incapable, and basically a failure and loser in life.

One of the basic solutions to this problem is having him enter school when he is ready, and not making him enter based on only his chronological age. This is the basic reason why the school administrations will sometimes recommend that kids repeat kindergarten. However, it is very difficult for parents to understand how their own kid can "flunk kindergarten" when he is really not being exposed to that much in academics. What they fail to realize is that this child needs a little more time to catch up to others. He is behind in development and thus needs to start a bit later in order to be on an equal level. It has nothing to do with intelligence, but is a matter of simple immaturity for his age, which will eventually pass. Taking care to understand this need can spare a lifetime of grief for the child. He will just move and develop on a slower time clock than others, but given some extra time, will be right where others are with minimal damage to his personal self-image. Time is on his side.

The Slow Learner

The problem with the slow learner is that although he struggles very hard, may be conscientious and not fool around in class, he just simply catches on very slowly. He would do a lot better if he could, but somehow he can't.[2]

The problem here is that he has a *lower intelligence level* and is therefore less able to grasp the concepts that he is bombarded with at school. He just does not absorb as quickly as others. He never gets 100 on his tests, no matter how hard he tries. He never gets the praise of the teacher, his parents, or his peers. He may be called "retard, dummy." He will very easily develop an inferiority complex and will tend to lag socially, as well as academically. He is the one who is always chosen last in everything. His age and size will work against him as he gets further and further behind in his work. Other kids will ask, to his embarrassment, why he is older but still in a lower grade. With this child, time is not on his side as he will never have the capability of catching up to others.

The solution for this child is somewhat different. He has been struggling very hard for standards and goals he cannot reach. For him, the goals need to be *reduced* somewhat, and he needs to be given things to do that are within his ability range. He needs to have work that is more on his level and thus learn that he can do something and be successful, even if it is not quite what others can do. For him, the hope of being the same as others is somewhat unrealistic.

He needs a specially designed program aimed toward some successes which will include the following:

1. *Teach him to read.* Even if he has to have one-

to-one teaching, extra tutoring, or special reading classes, do whatever it takes. Reading is very basic to all learning, and this skill he must gain.

2. *Shield him from unnecessary failure.* Have him work on assignments and projects that are within his level or his own group. When he tries hard, give him praise and encouragement.

3. *Success breeds success.* Whenever possible, show confidence that he can do something. This helps his own sagging self-confidence. Give him reachable goals; praise him for his efforts; help him to find success with smaller goals, which will in turn stimulate him toward higher goals. All of us tend to act as others see us; therefore, positive feedback will help him to achieve more than he otherwise would.

The Underachiever

The underachiever is somewhat of a different breed yet.[3] His problem is definitely not the lack of academic ability because, if he puts his mind to it, he could easily be an A or B student. Instead, he is a D and F student, and gets the frequent comment, "You can do better." He has the intellectual ability, so why can't he do the work? One other ingredient is missing. In this case, *self-discipline* is absent. Instead of getting into his homework, he is distracted by TV, by cars passing on the street, by his dog, by numerous other possible distractions, and he just never gets his work done. He does not have the self-will and self-discipline to turn aside from these distractions and, as a result, gets very little done. He just seems to have a natural resistance to mental exercise.

A concerned parent needs to get at this problem as quickly as possible. Gross underachievement, if allowed to continue, can become a permanent part of his way of life to the extent that he never reaches his full potential. The parent may be tempted to panic and give him a blast of belittling comments which would curl anyone's hair. Or the parent may, in utter frustration, say, "If you fail, you will stay indoors all summer!" Or the parent may be tempted to just detach himself uncaringly. "If he wants to fail, then that's his business; let him fail." None of these approaches presents an adequate solution.

The answer to our problem can be found in one of the following two ways, or both combined:

1. *The parent may become very involved.* The parent can insist that all assignments be completed and can request regular feedback from the schoolteacher to check to see if they are done. The parent can insist on specific study time without interruption, whether the child claims he has homework or not. The parent can insist on helping his child study for tests by reviewing with him, asking questions about the material, or making him write down important facts, all to help him retain information. This of course requires a lot of time and diligence to keep the whole thing on the track.

2. *Use a system of positive reinforcement.* The second thing the parent can do is to use a system of immediate reinforcement for developing study habits, somewhat similar to the method described in Chapter Eight, "Tools for Developing Maturity." Obviously, up to this point the usual incentives have not been enough. The thrill of getting 100 on a test, or the satisfaction of having done his best, have not been sufficiently experienced to become proper motivation in themselves. Some additional methods are needed. The use of rewards, such as money or a desired privilege, some family fun, or anything appropriate that the child desires, can be used to help increase motivation. A certain amount of monetary reward can be given for completing a unit of assignment, or for studying one hour in a needed area; or so many points can be awarded toward a desired goal. Again, remember that if points are given toward a larger goal, there needs to be some visual aid to help the child see how he is progressing. Reward him only for successes.

With the proper system of incentives a child will begin to learn more, simply because he is exposing himself to more of the material he needs to learn. After a while, the normal incentive of getting good grades and doing well takes over, and the artificial motivations are no longer needed. The situation becomes restored to normal.

The Strong-Willed Child

The strong-willed child is somewhat different in that he is the kind who never takes "no" for an answer. He is the child who will purposely do the very thing you've instructed him not to do. He is a rule bender from the day he is born, and will try in every way to bend, change, modify, soften, weaken in order to get away with whatever he can. The child will repeatedly take his parents to the brink. He will push further and further until the parent is finally ready to explode. At this point, he will do what he's asked.

Actually this child does not want his parents to give in, as he would lose respect for them if they did. He wants to be kept on the track, and will seldom go very far beyond the basic rules that his parents have laid down. He is locked into an ongoing conflict of the wills with his parents. Although he continually tries to win out, actually he is not comfortable with winning. He would rather the parent keep the control because he does not have a firm grasp of his own impulses.

Such a child can drive any parent up the wall numerous times per day. Possibly this type of child has inspired the bumper sticker, "Insanity is hereditary; you get it from your kids."

The solution in dealing with this type of child lies in a *careful balance* of *love* on one side, and *firm control* and structure on the other. Dr. Dobson's list of ingredients to such an approach is helpful:

1. Give a *clear* statement of what is required, and *carefully define the boundaries* at which the child can start and stop. Clear and definite instructions are very important to this type of child.

2. When challenged by this child, respond with *quick* and *affirmative action*. If the parent does not act decisively and quickly, the opportunity is lost and a battle of the wills quickly follows. With younger kids, a swat on the rear can be appropriate. With older kids, try a loss of privileges, or possibly some time out alone in his room until he gets his attitude back in shape.

3. The parent must *distinguish* between what is *willful defiance* and what is *immaturity* and act accordingly.

Deal with defiance straightforwardly, quickly, and with appropriate action, as already described. Deal with immaturity by teaching, explaining, encouraging, and reminding.

4. Give *reassurance* and explain the main point you're trying to teach the child after a confrontation has taken place. The statement, "Because I said so," may be appropriate to establish authority for the moment and may be necessary during the confrontation. However, after the confrontation, when things have settled down somewhat, it is appropriate to explain to a child why action was necessary.

5. *Avoid impossible demands.* Do not ask a child to do something that he cannot really accomplish or that is beyond his ability.

6. *Let love be your guide.* Have at all times a heart of compassion and a sense of knowing when you may be going too far or when you may need a bit of softening in your approach.[4]

I would also add: *Do not let your child run the home.* Too many parents are giving in to their children's manipulations simply to keep peace in the home. The parents' position becomes weaker and weaker and the child's demands only grow greater as time passes. This situation simply leads to greater chaos and upheaval during the teen years.

The parent must take charge. Parents who do not take charge are inviting disrespect and defiance from their kids and all the grief and heartache that follow. A home that is divided, in which the father feels one way about how things are to be dealt with, and the mother a different way, leads to an even greater sense of confusion in the home and greater comtempt and disrespect by the child who loves to play one against the other to get what he wants. Far too many homes deteriorate into chaos and then final disintegration because the parents allow disruption in their homes. Eventually their own marriage is destroyed by their children. Parenthood is a God-given responsibility which every parent must grasp firmly. The parent must be captain of his own ship and require a disciplined crew or the ship will drift, run aground, or possibly sink altogether.

The Scriptures present a two-sided approach to

this problem: one of shaping the will, and the other of preserving the spirit.

a. *Shaping the will*. In speaking of the qualifications of an elder or overseer, 1 Timothy 3:4, 5 says, "He must manage his own family well and see that his children obey him with proper respect. (If anyone does not know how to manage his own family, how can he take care of God's church?)" Scripture makes it distinctly clear that the parent, and the father in particular, is directly responsible for maintaining the authority of the home by *requiring* obedience from his children. It is no one else's job.

b. *Preserving the Spirit*. Ephesians 6:4 tells us, "Fathers, do not exasperate your children; instead, bring them up in the training and instruction of the Lord." This passage suggests that the father must not only give training and proper instruction, but also warns about going too far with strictness, scolding, or nagging so as to drive his child to desperation.

Minimal Brain Dysfunction

Some children are totally different than any described above. They have a special type of problem that may give them many different types of difficulties in school, home, community, or all of the above. The child may be classified as neurologically impaired or perceptually impaired, hyperactive, hyperkinetic, or learning disabled by a child study team. This child may be dealing with such problems as seeing letters of the alphabet reversed, seeing whole words reversed or changed in a sentence, double vision, difficulty with eye-to-hand coordination, inability to understand pictures, and inability to handle things; or terrible coordination, such as being unable to catch a ball or swing a bat, or just simply dropping everything. He may exhibit other symptoms such as disruptive behavior in the classroom, getting out of his seat, calling out in class, throwing temper tantrums over small things, showing hyperactivity by being constantly in motion, being very impulsive, quickly changing moods, or more severe behavior problems.

A problem like this requires special diagnostic evaluation tools and a special approach to correct behavior.

However, it should be understood that even though this child is having a very difficult time learning in school, he still may be very intelligent, and may be trying very hard. This problem is something he was born with. It is organic in origin, and is in no way created by the home environment. What causes this abnormality is somewhat unclear, but seems to be the result of underdevelopment of a small area of the brain. Whatever that part of the brain controls, whether it be coordination, visual perception, auditory perception, mathematical concepts, or whatever, that particular ability is grossly affected.

With careful diagnosis based on extensive testing for such things as learning disabilities, psychiatric evaluation, possibly neurological evaluation, and social history of the child's development, a more specific focus of the problem can be found, and a specific plan of treatment can be prescribed. Particular areas of needed development can be focused, and special time and effort given in a small group or on an individual basis to help this child develop in the specific area of need. This may include a special reading class, a special math class, or special neurological exercises, depending on his particular needs.

A great deal of firmness, short-range structure, and rather strict behavior requirements are essential to help this child gain the behavioral self-control he does not have for himself. Occasionally, the children with more severe problems of this nature may require residential schooling in which they have the availability of very specialized teaching to deal with their specific problem areas, as well as stricter behavior controls than the parent is able to provide.

The good news is that, with the proper help and guidance, these kids generally turn out reasonably well. Even though they have scraped through school, not paying attention, neglecting to turn in assignments, and never showing any real interest, some of these kids begin to show an interest in secondary school and demonstrate the ability to work hard. Some may want to go on to some form of further training. The extra curricular activities of high school may help spark that interest. Other kids may not show any change of interest and may continue to be at odds with anything to do with school. A varied program of vocational subjects and some work-study programs help these youngsters to complete high school. Most of these kids will go into the various vocational trades and can lead a reasonably normal life. Further education may hold no interest at all, but a decent living can and is being made by many who have learned to work hard at something they can do and are interested in. The parent must have realistic expectations for each child, and not try hard to push kids beyond their limits.

The following list of symptoms of hyperactive children gives you some idea of the types of things to look for. Consider it normal if your child has a few of these symptoms. If he has most of these symptoms clustered together, then it would be advisable for you to seek a full evaluation and professional help. This could result in saving years of family misery, your learning how to handle this kind of child, and the child reaching his own potential much sooner without undue damage to his personality.

For preschool children:

1. Does your child stay up half the night playing and then wake up at the crack of dawn so that you hardly get any sleep yourself?

2. Is he far more active, restless, and energetic than other children his age?

3. Does his attention span seem much shorter than that of other children his age?

4. Does he throw temper tantrums for trivial reasons and do this regularly and often?

5. Is he so hard on things that he has worn out or broken his playpen, crib, or tricycle?

6. Is he persistently impulsive, running into the street, playing with electrical sockets, jumping from dangerous places like the top of the refrigerator, or drinking household cleaners?

7. When he is outside, do you have to supervise him much more closely than the other parents on the block watch their children, for fear he will run off or do something wild?

8. Does he bite, kick, and scratch other children, or attack them often?

9. Is he unusually willful and disobedient?

For school-age children:

1. Is it very hard for him to be still? Does he seem to have boundless energy?

2. Does his attention span seem much shorter than that of other children his age, especially for things requiring an effort?

3. Does he talk, fidget, rock, drum his fingers a lot?

4. Do his emotions swing rapidly from excitement to anger? Does he cry easily and often?

5. Is he hard to get to bed at night?

6. Does he continually get up from the table or play during mealtimes?

7. Is he having trouble in school, either with his academic work or because of his behavior?

8. Does he usually leave projects unfinished?

9. Does punishment seem to have no effect on his behavior?

10. Does he seem unhappy much of the time? Is he whiny and irritable? Does he complain that "no one likes me"?[5]

A number of special problem areas have been identified and outlined. Should you need further help with your child, do not hesitate to enlist the services of a trained family counselor who can help you and your child get a better grasp on life before a lot of damage is done to the individual, and before a lot of unnecessary unhappiness is perpetuated within the home. There are trained people who have a definite gift for helping, and certainly there is no shame in any parent seeking help.

Workbook Section Chapter Nine

1. *Symptoms.*

My child shows the following problems with school and home as described in this chapter:

_____   _____
_____   _____
_____   _____
_____   _____
_____   _____

This tells me he/she has some of the symptoms of the:

_____ late bloomer
_____ slow learner
_____ underachiever
_____ strong-willed child
_____ minimal brain dysfunction child

2. *Approach to the problem.*

From what I learned from this chapter, my child will respond best to the approach most suited to his needs. He needs the approach that emphasizes:

_____
_____
_____
_____

As I think over the approach that we have been using, I can see we have been doing some things right, and need further work on some others. Some of the things we have been doing right are:

_____   _____
_____   _____

_____   _____
_____   _____
_____   _____

     Some ways that we need to strengthen our approach are:

_____   _____
_____   _____
_____   _____
_____   _____
_____   _____

     We may have not been fully realistic in all our expectations, and can see that we need to pull back a bit by:

_____

_____

[1]Dobson, *Discipline*, pp. 133-138.

[2]*Ibid.*, pp. 138-148.

[3]*Ibid.*, pp. 148-159.

[4]James Dobson, *The Strong-Willed* Child (Wheaton, Ill.: Tyndale House Publishers, 1978), pp. 31-33.

[5]Mark A. Steward and Sally Olds Wendkos, *Raising a Hyperactive Child* (New York: Harper and Row Publishers, 1973), pp. 36, 37.

Ten

Dealing with Teens

"I don't understand what is happening to my child. He was always so willing to help out before, and always had a pleasant disposition. Now he is moody, mouthy, disrespectful, and leaves a trail of his personal belongings wherever he goes. He doesn't seem to care. What has happened?"

"My teenager criticizes me for everything I do. She calls me unfair, says that I don't love her, says I'm a sloppy housekeeper, and that she's embarrassed to bring her friends over, on and on and on. I'm fed up with the whole thing."

"My kid is tyrannizing my home. He is shouting, screaming, and always threatening about something. Every day it's another battle. It can be over anything, such as clothes not washed, not liking the dinner, staying out late, on and on. There's no reasoning with him. Every day is one big hassle. Some days I feel like just throwing him out, bag and baggage, but I could never forgive myself if I did. Is there no end to this?"

"We used to be a close family. We did everything together. Now my teenager doesn't seem to want to be bothered with us. He is always out with his friends and doing other activities, regardless of what we have to do or want to do together. What's wrong with us? Home has become more like a filling station where he pops in and out for food, clothes, and a bed at night, and that's it. What's happening to our family?"

"My adolescent girl is standing before the mirror

and saying things like, 'I'm ugly. I hate myself.' I've tried to reassure her that she's always been my cute little girl, but nothing helps. She continues to down-rate herself and be down on adults no matter what we do."

Puberty has struck again!

What brings about such abrupt and confusing changes, even in the best of homes? To understand what is happening, we must comprehend some basic growth changes that are taking place beginning in early adolescence, beginning approximately at age twelve. Some begin before this age, and some start a bit later.

Developmental Changes

1. *Physical changes.* A number of physical changes are happening in the body of an early adolescent. Just as with younger children, there were times of calmness and peaceful adjustment, as well as periods of fits and starts as the child expanded into new horizons toward the next level of achievement—the same pattern is likewise true of the teenager. He is experiencing rather rapid changes in his height in which many kids will shoot up quite rapidly. As a result, they suffer from numerous unexplainable aches and pains due to the rapid growth. He may be very gawky and uncoordinated. He may appear somewhat loosely thrown together with long legs and arms, and have large feet which continually fall over each other and get in each other's way. He may be suffering from acne or other ailments which mar his appearance. His reproductive organs will be developing. The girls will be filling out, and the boys will be showing signs of "peach fuzz" under the nose that vaguely resemble a mustache. Because of the extreme insecurity of his age, and because of his own disjointed appearance, he may be subject to numerous gibes from other kids which further complicate the confusion of the age. Girls will be extremely interested in such things as beauty, charm, poise—and boys. The boys will become interested in competitive skills, and cars and motorcycles, but girls come a bit later on the boys' list.

2. *Social changes.* Up to this point, the teenager has been quite happy to be a part of the family and an extension of the parents. But now he naturally begins to move

away from that closeness with his parents toward his own peer group to develop a group identity apart from his home. During this important intermediate step, acceptance by his peer group becomes vital. He feels tremendous pressure to conform to the wishes of the other kids, and finds it very hard to say "no" to them. If forced to make the choice between standing alone, which is terrifying, or belonging to a group with somewhat lower standards than those of his parents, he will in most cases choose to follow the group. A few will choose to be "loners" instead, but will need help to find alternate sources of friends such as a different church group, or an individual from elsewhere that shares a common interest.

3. *Emotional changes.* This is a time of extremes in moodiness between being very depressed and very hyper. The need for acceptance is extremely strong. The teen feels a lot of underlying inferiority at this age, and statements like, "I'm ugly" are very normal in the earlier teens. This is honestly how the teen views himself in his gawkiness and insecurity. Normally, this feeling changes within a year or two, and only becomes a serious problem if the teen fails to develop a more positive self-image.

The teen is also working through a lot of values concerning what is important to him and what is not. He is basically finding himself. He is looking for his own uniqueness as a person, as opposed to being a carbon copy of his parents. The child is breaking loose from his parents during this period toward being an individual in his own right. The initial breaking loose is a very confusing time; hence, the teen is no longer a child, but is not yet an adult. He vacillates back and forth between two positions until he gradually finds himself and his own personal identity. During this period he is likewise having a lot of problems with self-control. Angry outbursts are rather common, as are chronic complaints and irresponsible forgetting of things he needs to do.

There is just too much happening all at once for a teenager to be in full control of all phases of his life.

4. *Sexual development.* Not only is the teen developing in the physical aspects of his reproductive organs,

but a whole new set of urges, impulses, and interests come into play. He sees a girl on the street who never caught his fancy before, and suddenly there is a strange new awakening and magnetic pull toward her. He may not be fully sure what this is all about. He does know that when he is around her, or touches her, or spends time necking in the moonlight, a whole flood of new emotions come roaring through like a freight train, creating a lot of excitement that is hard to control. These powerful urges become their strongest at this time in life when he is least prepared to handle them. The teen needs a lot of help in self-control and appropriate behavior during this time.

5. *Changing spiritual values.* During this time, the teen is also accepting or rejecting his parents' religious values, and beginning to internalize those which are important to him or her. At this point, a firm belief in Christ as Savior and Lord can help greatly in the developing process of self-worth, as demonstrated by God's love for us in his Son's sacrifice and provision for eternal life. His own developing personal faith in God can be a great stabilizing influence during this very difficult time. Encourage personal daily Bible reading and church youth activities, as well as the open door to questions and discussion, but don't get preachy.

Meeting Teenagers' Needs

The basic need of every teenager is to have the opportunity to become a *self-sustaining, independent person able to make his own mature decisions according to his own internalized values.*[1] The parent can foster this kind of growth or hinder it, depending on the kind of relationship he develops during these important developmental years.

With all the things that are happening with the teenager, it is very easy to become *critical* of their behavior and their attitudes. They certainly give the parent plenty of opportunities. However, criticism will simply add to their confusion and already somewhat low self-esteem. Romans 14:13 tells us, "Let us stop passing judgment on one another. Instead, make up your mind not to put any stumbling block or obstacle in your brother's way." The spirit of judgment and criticism can be destructive to personal growth in others, especially to insecure teens.

The following are some of the ways in which fault finding can be destructive to a teen:

1. *Faultfinding communicates nonacceptance and a distorted view of reality.* The picture can easily be given to the teen that everything must be done perfectly or it is not acceptable; or worse yet, the teen himself is not acceptable. The teen is already struggling with the problem of acceptance and self-worth. A lot of faultfinding only makes that struggle more difficult.

2. *Criticism ruins human relationships.* Criticism is a direct attack on the person's self-worth and tends to foster mutual hostility and misery, first in the person giving the criticism, and second in the one receiving it. It hurts both the giver and the receiver. He may respond either by resentfulness, a counter attack, or simply by being "turned off" and not even listening to what is being said.

3. *Criticism is an ineffective way to change behavior.* The person simply becomes more defensive and builds the wall higher, with little desire to change. Too much criticism will dilute important messages that need to be spoken. The parent becomes the proverbial "broken record." When the parent does have something important to say to his teen, the message is lost before it is ever given.

4. *Frequent criticism teaches the teen intolerance and unreasonableness by example.* He may in turn become very much the same way himself.

5. *Faultfinding relies on a destructive defense mechanism.* The parent simply magnifies the faults of the other person, and as a result hides his own weaknesses. The teen is not fooled by this approach.[2]

Better results can be obtained by a more *positive approach* to dealing with problems of the teen. Some definite suggestions are listed.

1. *State the problem where possible.* Do not allow a problem to continue on and on with the resulting walls of resentment until the problem may then become too hard to deal with objectively. Ephesians 4:26, "Do not let the sun go down while you are still angry," is good advice in this situa-

tion as well as many others. Deal with problems the same day whenever possible.

2. *Deal with any problem with your teen in private.* The humiliation of being reprimanded in front of others is thus avoided, and the problem doesn't become unduly magnified in importance. The teen responds a lot easier, as he won't feel so defensive.

3. *Tell what you are pleased about.* Give as much positive reinforcement as you can, even though sometimes it may be hard to find. Look for effort that is being made or any particular area in which the teen has improved in some form. The recognition of positive effort gets the whole thing away from an "I'm always wrong" type of situation.

4. *Use "I" type statements, not "you" statements.* Stating the things that you as a parent are concerned about, rather than using direct attack language, will help relieve the tension. Avoid saying, "You're a sloppy bum because you leave everything lying everywhere." Try stating it in a more positive form: "I'm concerned about the fact that your personal things are left about, and that some will get lost or damaged. I would like you to try to make a definite effort to keep your things organized." A direct frontal attack is thus avoided.

5. *Deal with specific actions that concern you and avoid the pitfall of thinking that you know the other person's motives.* The teen may indeed be rude and indifferent, but may not intentionally be that way or even conscious of how he comes across. Call to his attention the specific attitude problem and deal with it. Don't assume that your teen is purposely out to drive you crazy or to treat you with disrespect. It may well have been accidental; but do deal with the problem.

6. *Do not compare your teen with the action and behaviors of others as proof of his own failings.* This only makes him feel more humiliated, and is really not a fair comparison. Every teen is an individual and does not need to be just like others.

7. *Forget the past and deal with the present issue.* The past is only useful as something to learn from, to leave behind, and to press on to newer and better things.

8. *Deal with one complaint at a time.* This is not a time to dump on your teen with a whole long list of things you have saved up over the past few months. The main point will only get lost in all the other things. Deal with only one at a time.

9. *Suggest some possible solutions to the problem being presented.* Other options often help the teen to figure out or see other ways he may never have thought of before. Training a teenager to discover options that help to relieve problems is invaluable to his future.

10. *Be sure to let your teen give feedback about his own feelings or suggestions.* Even if the teen reacts in anger, this is no call for the parent to give anger back. A parent simply needs to state, "Perhaps you don't see it this way as yet, but think about it, and try to make efforts to correct the problem."[3]

11. *Give your teen a firm example of responsibility demonstrated by both parents.* A teen who grows up in a home where the parents are frequently locked in emotional battles, where there is little or no direct communication, where love is not experienced and demonstrated, is a teen who is growing up in an emotionally deprived home. Every teenager needs the clear example of a mother and father who can deal with their problems rationally, talk them out, work out options, and reach conclusions in their thinking that can be useful. Every teen needs parents who are able to demonstrate love toward each other, as this promotes happiness and a sense of security about his own future marriage and the possibility of being happy likewise. Parents who are able to level with each other directly, without a lot of game-playing or restrained silence, teach the teenager that it is possible to deal with things very openly, and thus avoid a lot of heartache and pain.

12. *Give your teen a chance to learn to cope with life situations.* Life can easily appear to loom very large, threatening, and overwhelming to the teen. However, if he is taught by parental example and coaching to identify problems, and encouraged to look for alternative actions leading toward a definite solution, a teenager will thus be gathering the tools he needs to solve his problems and to cope with

life's situations. As he is able to take each new problem, work it through, and solve it in a reasonable way, he gains increasing self-confidence. As he gains more confidence, he takes on new challenges with greater gusto rather than shrinking from threatening situations.

Well-meaning parents who try to protect their teens from all the possible dangers of life, or to avoid all the heartaches that they themselves have experienced, are often depriving their teens of some very valuable training and experiences as to what life is really all about. On the other hand, the parent who thrusts his teen out into the hard, cold world with very inadequate direction or support is not considering his teenager either, as he is quite unready to face all those things alone. The teen needs a lot of understanding and support, and a lot of help in gaining a sense of direction. Encourage the teen to handle as much of it as he can for himself, but be ready to lend a hand where that is needed.

The teen needs a lot of support from his parents to develop his own inner strengths. Since he is in an important stage when he is forming a lot of his own convictions and values, and comparing the values of his friends with those of his parents, he is beginning to make choices for himself. He should not be robbed of that opportunity, and he will need a large loan of stability from his parents to help him weather these important storms. An uncaring or an unstable home simply hinders that process.

Every teenager needs an opportunity to make mistakes and to learn for himself. Parents should avoid the repeated provoking of guilt or shame at the teen's errors. The important point should not be the emphasis on what was wrong, but on what we can learn from this experience to better equip us for the future. Herein lies the basic difference between training and punishment. Training strengthens for the future as well as teaches right from wrong; whereas, punishment may only deal with what is wrong. Training may include punishment as one of several forms of teaching.

13. *Be a resource person for your teen.* Encourage open communication with your teen so that he feels free to ask questions about things he is uncertain about. Questions about dating, partying, staying out late, sex, marriage, fam-

ily, careers, and problems with peers are all things that the teen needs to feel free to ask about and discuss with his parents.

Understanding what is going on with your teen is half the battle, and the foundation for whatever follows. Without adequate understanding, parents will make mistakes. The other half is finding effective ways of keeping the communication channels open, and working out problems as they come. The suggestions just presented should help you accomplish this task.

"Wisdom is supreme; therefore get wisdom. Though it cost all you have, get understanding" (Prov. 4:7).

Workbook Section Chapter Ten

1. Teen development.
My teen is having adjustment problems in these areas (check where appropriate):
_____ physical adjustment
_____ social adjustment
_____ emotional stability
_____ sexual adjustment
_____ spiritual growth
Some things that I am particularly concerned about in my teen are:

_____
_____
_____
_____

2. Teen's special needs.
As I try to meet the needs of my teen, I think that I am (doing OK, or have a problem) in the following areas. Check as appropriate.

Doing OK	Parental Actions	Problem Area
_____	1. Critical attitudes	_____
_____	2. Discussing problems straightforwardly	_____
_____	3. Discussing problems privately with my teen	_____
_____	4. Telling him what I am pleased with	_____
_____	5. Admitting my own shortcomings as a parent	_____
_____	6. Not trying to guess my teen's motives without asking	_____

_____   7. Not comparing my teen to others   _____
_____   8. Not throwing up past problems   _____
_____   9. Dealing with one problem at a time   _____
_____   10. Living as an example of   _____
                  responsibility
_____   11. Giving my teen a second   _____
                  chance when he fails
_____   12. Trying to treat him as an adult   _____
_____   13. Answering questions directly and   _____
                  giving explanations why some things
                  must be as they are
_____   14. Reasoning with my teen on an   _____
                  adult level instead of as a child
_____   15. Giving him enough freedom to ex-   _____
                  perience a few mistakes in order
                  to learn for himself the hard way

   Look at the areas where you did well. Congratu-
late yourself, and thank God for his help and wisdom along
the way.
   Look at the areas where you need improvement.
As you think and pray about it, what are some definite things
you could do to improve the situation? Write these down in
the space below. Pick one out that you really want to work
hard on this week.

_____
_____
_____
_____
_____
_____

   [1]Norman Wright, *An Answer to Parent-Teen Relationships* (Irvine, Cal.: Harvest House Publishers, 1977), p. 5.

   [2]*Ibid.*, pp. 17-19.

   [3]*Ibid.*, pp. 20, 21.

Eleven
Teens and Authority

Changing Parental Roles
The type of parent needed for training teenagers is somewhat different than for younger children. Some parents will find the adjustment easier than others. The parent is no longer dealing with a young child that has to be watched at all times and told most things to do. The parental relationship to the teen is much closer to a one-on-one equal relationship, while still assuming the basic parental authority. This time can be a very confusing one for parents, but with the right approaches it can be a very rewarding time as well.

Parental Blocks
James Dobson, a prominent Christian psychologist, indicates *three basic parenting* styles that can become *problems* in raising teens.[1]

1. *Overharshness.* Severe strictness or punitive measures for a small infraction brings a great deal of inner humiliation to the teenager by the total domination of his life by the parent figure. The result is that the teenager is unable to make his own decisions, only because he's never been taught how, and a strong fear of making a wrong decision appears. He is taught to be very dependent on the authority of the parent, but overwhelming hostility grows within. The characteristics of dependency, hostility, and even possible psychosis may linger for years.

2. *Overpermissiveness.* The parents who just let their kids face the world by themselves without direction or restriction are thrusting them out into a world they are unable to handle. This type of approach fosters undue pride,

selfishness, and basically produces a spoiled kid who is unable to give and take with others. It fosters anarchy and chaos in the home and may easily lead to a situation in which the teen is boss. It does not teach proper respect for the other person. The teen is unprepared for the outside world due to his inability to handle responsibility or authority, and he thus flounders for years to come.

3. *Parental division.* An even more difficult situation is that of a serious division between the father and mother in the management of their children. One parent may be extremely permissive, and the other extremely restrictive. One may be very affectionate and the other very cold. The parents are in constant conflict because of their approaches. The end result is that the teen growing up in this atmosphere learns to respect *neither* parent for their attacks upon each other. He may even learn a manipulative relationship in which he will get what he wants by playing one parent against the other and thus divide the mother and father more completely, increasing their own conflict. A child growing up in this kind of home is a time bomb with a fuse lit, and often produces a most aggressive and belligerent teenager.

There are other blocks that get in the way of effective parenting with teens. *Smoldering resentments* on the part of one or both parents teaches the teen to avoid closeness with that person, or makes him fear taking sides. Thus he may remain aloof from both parents. This situation obviously closes off the needed communication, and the teen has to turn outwardly to others for his resources. "I can't talk to my parents," he will say. The tension in the home may encourage him to be absent as much as possible, which opens other doors for further difficulty. This way he is forced to seek out his own devices, and thus misses the valuable support that his parents could be to him during these important years.

Another block that parents face is *guilt for their own past actions.* Many parents experience difficulties, particularly from sowing their wild oats in their own teen years, or from severe adjustment problems and home difficulties. Some may have simply grown up in a lot of poverty and deprivation of a more physical nature. Many times the parent will try to overcompensate for his own past by going too far the opposite direction with his own teens. He or she may become too restrictive of the teen for fear of the teen slipping into the same errors the parent experienced in his own teen years. Or the parent may be far too permissive in reaction to his own restrictive home atmosphere. The parent coming from a poor background may tend to give too many material things to his or her teens without helping them to learn the value of earning things for themselves. The overcompensation is frequently no better than the original problem from which the parent is trying to protect his own kids. And often times it will create the same or other problems within his kids.

Another parental block is the *inability to trust.* The parent may be well aware of the many temptations and difficulties facing his teen, and may show a lack of trust by constant questioning, unwarranted disbelief of the teen's explanations, and the constant seeking of reassurance that the teen is doing the right thing. A teen who is trying very hard to do what is right, but is constantly mistrusted, eventually loses confidence in himself and the motivation to do the right thing. He will feel that there is no profit in doing good because he only gets the third degree for it anyway, so why not do the things that he is being suspected of? For example, an untrusting parent can easily jump to conclusions that his daughter has become sexually involved if she is an hour late in coming home from a date. Facts may not warrant this conclusion at all, and the teen is frustrated by the barrage of false accusations and names that follow.

Another block may be *undue expectations* of the teen from the parent's point of view. The parent may be demanding all A's in school, membership in the honor society, and definite plans for college which may not fit the teen's capabilities or interests that well at all. This also can bring a great deal of frustration, a sense of failure, or outright rebellion.

Teen's Needs Are Different
Each teen has certain *positive needs*. One of his basic needs is *respect for his present position in life*. It is far

more important for a teen to feel a part of the grade he is in than to think of being the president of some large industrial conglomerate. He wants to feel that he is an accepted part of his own current school, home, and community groups, rather than living in some faroff dream that does not realistically fit him. He needs to be respected as an individual in his own right and no longer as a child who needs to be told every little thing. He needs the kind of respect that gives him a chance to do some thinking on his own, to ask questions, to explore, to experiment within reasonable limits, to be listened to when he has a complaint, and to be asked for his own opinion about things.

A teen needs to have a feeling that he has some *personal privacy.* In his developing individualism, he needs some time alone and a place that he can call his own, preferably a room to himself, if possible. He needs to be allowed to close the door, play his own music, and be free to do things that he wants within the basic framework of the household values. The parents should not be insulted when he prefers to stay home while they go out on a family outing, or when he prefers the company of his friends instead of being with them. This is a normal part of his development.

Every teen needs an *open channel of communication* with the family, with either of the parents alone or together. He needs the ability to express himself, his thoughts, and his views, although the parents may not agree with them. Instead of being quick to condemn, the wise parent will encourage his teen to express himself, and then help him to think through the further-reaching consequences of his own views, opinions, and choices. By being helped to think things through, the teen is gaining valuable experience in learning how to solve problems and direct his own life by adequate thought, rather than by impulsive action. This sort of open channel encourages the teen to ask questions or discuss problems with reference to issues which are very important to him, such as morals, drugs, alcohol, dating, sex, careers, problems with friends, concern about world problems, and many other things that are whirling around in his mind.

Parental Anxieties

Dr. Roy W. Menninger has made some helpful suggestions to assist parents in dealing with some of the anxieties of parenthood that go with raising teens.

1. *A parent should not let his own feelings of inadequacy get to him.* Every parent has doubts about himself at times. It is quite normal for the parent to wonder if he is handling things in the right way. The fact that the parent is asking this question indicates that he is functioning as a parent as he should in looking for the best way to resolve problems.

2. *The parent should not let a certain amount of family friction discourage him.* Disagreement, even though sometimes loud, is still a form of communication. The friction of unpleasant communication is still better than indifference and cold silence. This leaves opportunity to iron some things out. A certain amount of conflict is important to the teen's developing his own self-image apart from his parents.

3. *A parent should not be afraid of himself or his own values and life styles.* Even if his children seem to turn against his values, he should still stick with his own standards, as the kids actually want this.

4. *Don't mistake a passing personality phase for a permanent problem.* When a child no longer seems to confide as easily and naturally once he reaches age fourteen, this can very well be a temporary stage, and the parent who struggles too hard to change that may be making everybody miserable in the process.

5. *Don't blame the permissiveness on this generation.* This is a dangerous oversimplification which implies that the remedy is the exact opposite, the repression of authoritarianism. No extreme is better than any other extreme.

6. *The parents should resist the temptation to react with anger and withdrawal toward a difficult child.* Actually the so-called "difficult child" is often the one who needs the patience and understanding, and does not want to shut his parent out. He may simply need some help in gaining self-control over his behavior at that point.[2]

Discipline Problems

Discipline with a teenager must be handled differently. Attempts to spank or use physical punishment in any form only build deeper resentment, antagonism, and rebellion. No teenager wishes to be treated like a little child. On the other hand, no teenager should be allowed to roam freely about and do what he pleases, when he pleases. Every home must have definite standards that are insisted upon as reasonable behavior and expectations.

Rules are aimed at:

> keeping adequate control and order in the home
> teaching respect for authority
> training for the future

Rules can become teaching tools, particularly if their purpose is explained. The way they are presented is very important. The parents should not present rules to be obeyed simply because "I said so," as this is rarely an adequate reason for the teenager. The approach should be instead, "Come, let us reason together." It often helps to involve your teenager in the setting up of reasonable rules. This helps the teen to view the rules as partly his own, and he does not feel as restricted or resentful toward them.[3] Some sample rules for home might be things such as the following:

1. Have respect toward parents.
2. Have respect for parents' beliefs, values, and standards.
3. Give information as to where he is and when he will be home, and the reasons.
4. Take care of his own room by keeping it reasonably neat, clean, and organized.
5. Help with certain chores in the home without chronic complaining.
6. Some definite expectations concerning use of the family car when that becomes appropriate, including sharing in expenses.
7. Proper attention to achievement in school according to his or her ability.

Contracting

Sometimes particular problem areas can be worked out by *contracting*. This is basically an agreement, usually written, in which the teen will agree to do certain things in return for a reward. Failure to carry out the contract on either side will cancel the agreement. For example, a teenager may wish to have a stereo, a ten speed bike, some extra clothes, or a lot of other such tangible items. In an attempt to teach the teen some responsibility and the value of money, the parent may often prefer not to just give teens money or possessions, but will work out an agreement whereby the teen may earn the money by doing certain things. Money can be earned by doing certain jobs around the house; or it could be given as a way of helping the teen improve his reading ability. For instance, by requiring that he read a certain number of books within a set amount of time, each worth a certain amount of reward dollars, he could be encouraged to save up money to be applied toward the desired object. This approach has several advantages:

1. It relieves the parents of the burden of giving everything to the child, which they may not really be able to afford.
2. It teaches responsibility to the teen in working toward goals and successfully reaching them.
3. It gives the teen a sense of accomplishment and value for himself as a person, and a sense of value for the item he has earned.

If the desired item happens to be on sale and there is a definite advantage in purchasing it before the goal is reached, you may advance the money. But limit the usage of the item until the full amount is paid off. This, in essence, is a contract between the parent and his teen. It may be verbal if there is good communication between parents, but is often preferably done in a written form, signed by both. It is very important that a teenager not be given the goal if he does not earn it; and likewise, it is very important not to deny or post-pone a goal once it has been earned. Both parties must stick closely to their agreement.

In Chapter Eight, an example was given of a similar way of accomplishing the same things through points awarded for certain privileges or desired items. A sample contract chart was also given. For instance, if a teen wishes to purchase a cassette tape recorder, he must earn a certain number of points, say 1,000, in the next six to ten weeks to earn this privilege. The list can be as follows:

1. For making the bed and straightening the room each morning — 5 pts.
2. For each hour of study — 15 pts.
3. For each hour of house or yardwork — 30 pts.
4. For being on time at meals, morning and night — 5 pts. each meal
5. For baby-sitting his younger siblings — 15 pts./hr.
6. For washing the car each week — 25 pts.
7. For rising at 8 o'clock on Saturday morning — 10 pts.

Once the teen has reached the total, in this case 1,000 points, he is awarded the desired item.

There is no one set way to handle the contracts, and you must be adaptable to the needs of each teen and the situation at hand.

Unreasonable Behavior

Unreasonable behavior must be dealt with directly. A teen who becomes belligerent and who is emotionally out of control needs to be sent to his or her room for a *cooling-off period* until such a time as he or she is ready and able to be civil and discuss things properly. The amount of time necessary may have to be varied according to the type of child. Or it may be simply and clearly expressed to the child that he is not welcome back into the family circle until such a time as he is ready to become a part of it again. This can often be an effective means of helping the teen to calm down.

Very definite violations of previous agreements, such as coming home an hour late without any calls or explanations, may be dealt with by withholding the TV or some other desired privilege for several hours in the evening. Larger infractions, such as being suspended from school, or not attending classes, may require grounding from activities for a period of several days (but not to exceed a *maximum* of two weeks, preferably one week). By the end of the first week the teen no longer remembers very clearly why he is being grounded, and he begins to resent the restrictiveness put upon him. This may cause him to rebel all the more.

The parent will find that many of the same manipulative devices mentioned in Chapter Six are also being used by the teen (and by some adults as well).

Delaying — Never getting to the task so that the parent in exasperation finally does it for him.

Ignoring — Acting like nothing was ever said in hopes the parent will forget what he is asking.

Whining — "That's too hard." Seeking self-pity so that the parent will do the task himself.

Wearing down — Persistent questions or resistance until the parent gives up in exhaustion.

Forgetting — When excessive, in hopes the frustrated parent will do it himself.

Outright defiant refusal — A direct challenge to the parent's authority, hoping the parent will back off.

Tantrums — Yelling and screaming, general uproar, in hopes the parent will become sidetracked and back off.

Guilt trips — Attempts to make the parent feel unfit or ashamed because none of the teen's friends "have any such requirements."

Each of these manipulations must be dealt with directly and firmly, and the parent should not allow himself to be conned by any of them. Make it clear what is to be done, and follow through to see that it is done.

Keep in perspective at all times, that the main purpose of insisting that things are to be done is not to make your load easier, as you could do the task easier yourself. You are preparing your teen for life, and by insisting on his completing reasonable tasks, you are teaching him:

responsible behavior
respect for authority

Without these two qualities, no teen will be prepared for adult life that is just around the corner.

Parents' Resources

This can be a time of severe testing and certainly a time that requires growth in all parents. It is important that the parent has his own inner resources and time alone away from the hassle, and time to relax and get his own life back into perspective. No one can deal with the constant strain day by day without a letup and not feel the effects of it in irritableness, impaired judgment, and the general feeling of frustration and misery.

A parent should also draw very heavily upon his spiritual resources in the Word of God and his personal relationship with the living Lord. These will bring the parent the encouragement, inner peace, and stability that he or she needs. The parent should keep in perspective that "This too shall pass away," and that one day he can look back and say, "It was worth it all." Parents who are able to keep the whole period of time in perspective, deal with the problems on a day-to-day basis, and work them out as best possible will reap great rewards themselves and within their own children in years to come.

Romans 12:1, 2 gives us the heart of the growing, transforming process into full adulthood. It teaches the teen the following principles:

1. Complete surrender to God in place of surrender to peer pressure and this world system. A day-to-day renewal is needed.
2. Following behavioral standards that are outlined in his guidebook; for example, the book of Proverbs. A day-to-day effort.
3. Renewed thinking. The inner thoughts of the heart, plans, purposes, are all redirected in a new way on a day-to-day basis.
4. These steps bring a transformation of life in the right direction, and the teen who has been walking in these steps will demonstrate the will of God in his daily living.

Workbook Section Chapter Eleven

1. Parenting style.
As a parent I can see that I have been:
_____ overly harsh
_____ overly permissive
_____ undermining my spouse
_____ using a reasonable balance of all these

2. Parental sensitivity.
As a parent I try to relate well to my teen, and (am doing OK, or have problems) in the following areas. Check as appropriate.

Doing OK	Parental Actions	Problem Area
_____	1. Modeling closeness of relationships at home	_____
_____	2. Separating my teen's needs from my own past problems	_____
_____	3. Not blaming this generation for all the world's troubles	_____
_____	4. Not withdrawing in anger but dealing with every situation equally and fairly	_____
_____	5. Maintaining some reasonable requirements that I will insist upon	_____
_____	6. Requesting that he earn some of his own spending money to learn responsibility	_____
_____	7. Letting him be with his friends instead of always requiring him to be with the family	_____

_____   8. Basically trusting him as long   _____
                as there is adequate communi-
                cation, unless he proves otherwise
_____   9. Tolerating some of his moods as   _____
                "growing pains" but still
                setting some definite limits
_____   10. Respecting his right to privacy   _____
_____   11. Understanding his stages and   _____
                keeping an overall perspective
_____   12. Recognizing that some conflict   _____
                is natural
_____   13. Being firm in my stand on impor-   _____
                tant issues, but willing to bend
                when that is appropriate
_____   14. Providing an orderly and friendly   _____
                home that is open to my teen and
                his friends

How did you do? Are there some areas in which you did well? Good. Continue with those. Are there some areas in which you need improvement? Jot down some definite things you want to work on in the space below.

_____

_____

_____

_____

_____

_____

Put a star beside one that you really want to concentrate on this week, and go to it.

3. Contracting.

I can see where some contracting (verbal or written) could be very helpful in working out some problem areas with my teen. I know that he really wants to have

_____ .

I could help him work it out by setting up an agreement whereby he would (specify what and when):

_____

_____

_____

_____

_____

In return, I would pay him in (points, money, hourly rate) toward what he wants until he reaches his goal. I realize he must agree to this as well, and that we must have a clear, firm contract together.

[1]Dobson, *Discipline,* pp. 46-49.

[2]Roy Menninger, M.D., "How to Understand the Perplexing Teen-ager," *Reader's Digest,* Vol. 100, No. 599 (Pleasantville, N.Y.: Reader's Digest Association, March 1972), pp. 159-164.

[3]Jay Kesler, *Too Big to Spank* (Glendale, Cal.: Regal Books, G/L Publications, 1978), p. 64.

Twelve
The Parent as Counselor

"My child seems lonely and depressed. I asked her what is wrong, but I get the chronic reply, 'Nothing.' Things don't seem to change. What can I do?"

"My child's grades are going down in school. The teacher says that she daydreams a great deal and something must be bothering her. There is a problem somewhere, but I don't know where or what to do."

"My teenager is easily influenced by his other friends, and tends to choose the wrong kind of people for friends. I'm afraid he's headed for trouble, but I don't know how to get this across to him or help him to choose better friends."

"My teenage son has found a nice girlfriend, but I am concerned because they spend long hours together without very many plans and activities. I'm afraid that they will get into trouble in their personal relationship, but I don't know how to get this across without it being taken as an accusation or becoming a conflict."

"My daughter talks freely to other adults about her problems but she doesn't come to me. I don't understand. What do I need to do to gain her confidence?"

"How can I help my son overcome some of his obnoxious behavior? I'm sure some of the things he does give him problems with his friends, but I don't know how to do this without it appearing insulting to him."

There are times in the life of every parent when he realizes that his child is having a problem and wishes he could help. But many times, the door does not seem to be open for that. A parent who has a very open relationship with his or her child, in which the child feels free to share his joys and accomplishments, as well as problems and difficulties, has a very valuable relationship. Such a parent should consider himself very fortunate. What are the things every parent can do to develop an open relationship and become a confidential counselor to his own child?

Blocks to an Open Relationship

There are a number of things a parent can do, without even consciously thinking about it, that tend to block the kind of relationship in which he can be helpful to his own child. Let's look at a few of these.

1. *Panic reaction.* The parent coaxes the child to confess something he has done. With pain and embarrassment the child finally spills it out, only to have the parent react with hysteria. Examples of panic reactions are, "What will the neighbors think? I'll kill you. I hate you. How could you do this to me? I'll keep you in for a whole year!" Each of these represents a hysteria reaction with all the inappropriate screaming and shouting to go along with it. The child very quickly learns from this that it is easier to cover his own actions either by secretiveness or by lying, as truth only brings uproar and humiliation.

2. *Judgment and vindictiveness.* The parent can overreact with very severe punishments that are quite inappropriate to the situation, or overpunishment for things too minor to be considered that seriously, or an undue long period of being grounded. Cold silence or withdrawing of love also stifles the relationship and discourages further openness. One common problem is that of guilt games in which the parent blames the child for everything that goes wrong. If he has a problem in school with his friends, it is automatically the child's fault. If something goes wrong at home, it is automatically the child's fault. This approach gradually destroys the confidence of the child as well as the desired open relationship with the parents.

3. *Overrestrictiveness and overprotectiveness.* A refusal to let a child explain anything that has happened to him is a great mistake and leads to further blocks in communication. A parent who is very restrictive robs the child of

his own opportunity to develop his personal ability to explore life, to learn for himself, and to handle his own affairs appropriately. A parent who is watching out for the child to protect him from all harm is likewise robbing a child of his own chance to develop and learn by experience. This automatically presents the parent as the ultimate authority in all matters, conveying to the child the message that he has no ability at all, and therefore, there is no need for discussion.

4. *Wallowing in self-pity, guilt, and doom.* The parent who is always searching for an answer to the question, "Where did I go wrong?" is always searching for some fault within himself because of things the child is doing. The parent is robbing himself of his own self-respect and further blocking his channel of communication with his own child. The parent will feel quite inadequate to be of help to his child at this time, and the child will sense that inadequacy.

5. *Capitulation and defeat.* A parent who has given up and won't try and just slides along with whatever is happening, likewise closes himself off from his child. At this point, the parent is becoming somewhat dependent on the child to become the parent, to take responsibility for himself, and is basically conveying to the child that he has nothing to offer the child because he feels too incompetent himself. He will, therefore, block off the open communication that could be there and, by default, throw away his opportunity to be of help. The childish parent is likewise requiring his child to give up his own childhood needs in order to take charge of the helpless parent, a serious detriment to the normal development of the child.

All of these reactions tend to polarize the situation between parent and child and to drive problems deeper than they need to be. In contrast, there are certain steps that every parent can take in order to help encourage an open relationship with his or her children, which in turn makes it possible for the parent to be helpful as a counselor to his children.

Understand the Needs of Your Child
One very essential ingredient in developing an open relationship with your child is understanding the basic

struggles he is experiencing. As is pointed out in Chapter Seven, "Distinguishing Immaturity," every child is going through various stages of growth, physically, emotionally, and spiritually. The alert parent will familiarize himself with what the normal struggles are at the various age levels, and will encourage his child through these. Some of the basic developmental paths extending through most of the child's life, and particularly intensified during early adolescence, are outlined in the following paragraphs.

1. *Basic self-worth.* Every child is struggling to be important at his own age level. For a child of ten to be able to help his father in the yard in some tangible ways helps him to feel important as a boy of ten. For a father to take a son of fourteen on a fishing trip and to teach him to handle the boat does a great deal for the sense of worth and value of the boy as an individual. For a girl at age sixteen to be asked on a date for an important social event by a boy that she likes does something for her basic worth and value as an individual. She then feels attractive as an individual and wanted and accepted socially by others. For her to sit home alone while her friends are invited produces the opposite effect.

2. *Autonomy.* Every child is struggling with the ability to take charge of his own life in the midst of a somewhat bewildering world. That ability gives him a sense of independence, which in turn gives him confidence in his future ability to take charge of his own affairs. Just as it is important for a child of four or five to learn how to tie his own shoelaces as a part of that struggle for autonomy, or later to learn to ride a two-wheel bike, it is equally important for a seventeen-year-old to pass his or her driver's test and be allowed to use the family car with parental permission. Each of these is another step toward personal autonomy, the ability to take charge of one's own life in a responsible and appropriate way.

3. *The socialization process.* Just as it is important for a child of four or five to learn to play with other kids, cooperate in a group situation rather than grabbing all the toys for himself, or constantly making noise to disrupt everything, it is also important for every child to feel a part of the group process with his own age level, whether it be in

sports, games, skating parties, slumber parties, or dates in later teens. It is extremely important to feel wanted and accepted by one's own peer group, as well as to learn how to work out the problem areas that come up in any group. Conquering our disappointments, dealing with the intimidation or taunts of other kids, and earning one's place of respect is an important part of that struggle.

4. *Development of masculinity or femininity.* From roughly age five, boys and girls begin to discover their sex role characteristics. As girls play with dolls and boys play with trucks; as boys build clubhouses and girls have their tea parties; and as teenage boys become very interested in cars and motorcycles, and girls become interested in boys, the formulation of masculine and feminine roles in one's own development of sexual identity becomes another important struggle. The once clear masculine and feminine roles are today becoming increasingly fuzzy, as boys now learn to cook and girls to drive trucks. Thus, our kids need more help than ever to become comfortable with their masculinity as young men, or femininity as young women, and to develop their greatest potential in that framework.

Growing up to maturity means overcoming the blocks that get in the way of each of these developmental tasks. Anything which gets in the way will bring frustration, a sense of failure, and discouragement. The sensitive parent will be *aware* of the frustration, and will be *available* to help his or her child with any of those hurdles that become too difficult for the child himself to handle. Success in each of these developmental tasks will bring increasing confidence, increasing sense of worth, and increasing courage to try new and greater challenges. A child who is able to successfully meet each of these challenges throughout his growing up years will be able to face the realities and demands of life as an adult without undue difficulty. A child who meets with failure in one of these developmental tasks along the way will be blocked in that particular area of growth for some time, and will meet with an increasing amount of frustration and failure in life. Parents can give a tremendous amount of supportive help to a child in overcoming these various hurdles in the growing up years.

Demonstrate Acceptance and Understanding

A wise parent will try to gather all the facts before forming a judgment, or giving an authoritative opinion about what the child needs to do. Although children seem to be very perceptive in many situations, they are very naive in other areas and often form their own conclusions based on wrong assumptions or misinformation. It is important for the parent to try to understand the viewpoint of his or her child, even though the parent may disagree. It is important that the parent try to find out what else might be happening in a child's life, even though it seems unrelated to what the child is complaining about. For example, a child may be doing poorly in school. This is generally only a *symptom* and does not tell us the *source* of the real problem. The problem may simply be in not understanding the schoolwork, but it can also go to much broader proportions. A child may be struggling with relating to a teacher who is intimidating to the child; or the child may be struggling with a real problem in his peer group relationships in which he is receiving a great deal of teasing and rejection or is intimidated by a very threatening group of kids. His mind will be preoccupied with his problems, and he will find it very hard to concentrate on schoolwork. Problems at home such as parental conflict, loneliness because both parents are working or absent, or a situation not conducive to decent study habits will bring the same problems of concentration difficulty. The parent, therefore, needs to ask a few questions around these various areas to try to understand what else may be contributing to the whole picture.

It is also important to understand the situation of your child. Kids in today's world face tremendous pressures from their peers that most parents do not fully understand. Kids are faced daily with strong pressure to join in and experiment with drugs, alcohol, and sex. In many cases, they are facing these pressures almost daily, and most kids find it extremely hard to stand alone.

Many parents do not fully understand the kid's conflict of values. For what is very important to the parents may not hold the same importance to their teenager. For example, material things and community status may be important to you as a parent, but your child may not care the least about it. The opposite may also be true. The teenager may be interested in being a part of an "important family," whereas you're interested in a simpler life style. The parent may have the desire to see his kid go to college and "become something," whereas the teenage son may be more interested in a trade or a related vocation, which in the long run will just as adequately support a growing family and be personally fulfilling for him. Pressure for college in such a case meets the need of the parent more than the child.

A parent can easily overlook the personal frustrations and failures the child is experiencing because the parent is not that well in tune with what's going on with his child. It is very easy, likewise, for the parent to mistake symptoms for a real problem. For example, a child who complains a lot and who views himself as ugly or says that he hates himself may be simply reflecting his own feelings of personal worthlessness. At that point, simply refuting what the child has said is not the real answer to the problem, but parental efforts toward helping the child feel more worthwhile as a person are very much in order.

Throughout the years, as the child faces various hurdles, expression of love and affection by the parent is extremely important, and at no time should be neglected. A parent can be absolutely disgusted with his child's behavior, but needs to still be careful to express his love for the child as a person. The parent must avoid the equation, "If you're good, I will love you." Children often get this message and either join it or fight it in order to get attention of some sort. Assurance of love is needed. The parent who is sensitive to the needs of his child will find ways to show love without embarrassing the child. For instance, it is not the best idea for a loving mother to kiss her teenage son in front of his friends. He will be very embarrassed, his friends will be snickering up their sleeves, and he will face some razzing later. A father may feel a little uncomfortable about hugging his fifteen-year-old daughter who has now developed physically. However, there are ways of touching and hugging without sexual implications. The personal warmth of the parent must be evident at all times.

The parent must be careful to recognize the importance of self-esteem needs. When a child struggles with a difficult area, point out his strengths and help him discover resources that will give him further courage to overcome his problems and balance out his weaknesses. Every child needs to have an accurate view of himself, both of his strengths and his weaknesses in order to be accepting of himself, and have the courage to grow. Romans 12:3 tells us, "For by the grace given me I say to every one of you: Do not think of yourself more highly than you ought, but rather think of yourself with sober judgment, in accordance with the measure of faith God has given you." A healthy view of one's self gives the appropriate balance between pride in one's ability and accomplishment, and a humble spirit.

Learn to Listen

It has been said that God has given to each of us one mouth which can be closed and two ears which always remain open. However, most of us have the situation reversed: our mouth is never closed and our ears are never really open. *Listening is hard work,* and requires our concentration. But it is extremely vital to any open communication.

Communication is actually the conveying of *understanding* between two people. Communication is definitely *not* just thinking up words for the next reply, as words are simply the *ingredients* of a debate. When listening to your child, ask yourself the question, "What is my child really trying to tell me?" Try to hear what the child is feeling inside, such as frustration, anger, fear, rejection, helplessness, or rejoicing. Try to determine where the feeling is coming from and what the real problems are behind what is being said or done. From there, the parent can find a more appropriate way to help. Someone you love needs your help; figure out the best way to help under the circumstances. Without listening, you'll never get to that point.

Reason with Your Kids

Nothing will turn an adolescent off more than a lecture that goes on and on. He will simply learn how to tune it out, to let it go in one ear and out the other without any constructive learning. One very valuable thing a parent can do for his teenager is to help him *think through* the consequences of his or her behavior. Start with his situation, such as spending time with a group of kids on the street corner for several hours each night without any structured activities. Help him to think through the kinds of things that will begin to happen as the group looks for excitement and "just something to do." Help your teenage daughter to think through the consequences of spending too much time alone with her boyfriend, either in a car or in the house without another adult present. What sort of things are likely to happen, and what can be done to prevent them? If your child is complaining bitterly about the rules and regulations of school, ask him to think through what would happen if they removed all rules and regulations. What would be the result, what would school be like, what would he gain and what would he lose? Most kids are quick to see the answer, if you let them. They realize that chaos would result, and they would not have a situation in which they could learn and prepare themselves for life. If a child is given to telling a few lies here and there to cover up the things he wants to get away with, point out to him the longer range results of mistrust that follow, and how mistrust makes it very hard for a family to function in a loving, accepting way.

Sometimes your child has difficulty seeing where his own behavior presents a problem. Using a hypothetical example can be useful. For example, if your son tends to be loud, boisterous, and obnoxious, you may be able to describe a situation of how someone else might act in an obnoxious way. Then ask for his own reaction to that type of situation. It often helps the child to see how he really comes across to others, and how others view him. Roleplaying, in which the parent takes the role of the child or the child takes the role of the parent, can be very helpful in enabling your child to discover what's really happening between him and others.

Advice

Sometimes it is simply necessary for a parent to fill in some data. Take, for example, a teenager who is working and is asked to contribute a small amount toward the household expenses. Some teenagers have the idea that they are making their parents "rich." At this point, it is helpful for the parent to pull out a budget sheet and show what it really does cost for various things. Simple data as to how much it costs for electricity each month, for payments on the house, car, etc., often helps an adolescent to understand what life is all about, and that it isn't as simple as it first appeared. Data about colleges and careers, what they are like and what they involve, helps your child to make decisions for himself. Sometimes the parent needs to fill in some basic facts about the dangers of a certain behavior, as the child does not see it for himself. For example, kids do not get the full picture about drugs and alcohol from their peers, only the inviting aspects of it. A parent needs available data to show the other side of the picture. Kids sometimes get wrong information, such as the belief that a girl can get pregnant by kissing. Simple information helps to resolve such misconceptions, provided it is given in a proper spirit.

Develop a Trusting Relationship

Trust is a vital part of any relationship. There are a number of things that help to build this. One is simply truthfulness. A parent who is open and truthful with his own kids will tend to instill the same values in the child's life. The child learns from consistent truthfulness to trust his own parents, and by returning the same will invite trust from the parents as well. Lies, unfulfilled promises, and chronic inconsistency tend to undermine the relationship of trust.

Another part of trust is learning to respect each other's privacy. A child needs to be allowed to have a few secrets with his or her friends, just as the parent needs to be allowed a few private matters between husband and wife and other adults. As the child grows he should be given an increasing amount of privacy with his own things, his own diary, his own room, and his own private conversations. A parent who chronically goes through a child's drawers and letters and demands to know everything that is said, is putting his child on the defense, unnecessarily in most cases. By demonstrating mistrust, where that mistrust is inappropriate, the parent is teaching his child to do the same.

A parent must also learn to keep confidences. If a child opens up his inner feelings to the parent, the parent must be careful to keep that between him or her and the child and not make it known to others.

Do Things with Your Kids

Children will not naturally communicate openly with the parents unless there is a relaxed atmosphere in which they may feel free to speak. When a child comes home right after school that offers an excellent opportunity for the parent to listen constructively to the events of that day and to encourage discussion. The dinner table offers another place and time to share things as a family. But many parents are unaware of the fact that joint participation in some special event such as a game or activity together also frees a child to talk to his parents about something on his mind. A day spent fishing together, playing ball in the backyard, a special treat at McDonald's, or other things like this do a great deal to open up the communication between the parent and child.

These are times when the child feels he has one parent all to himself. It is *his* game, *his* snack, *his* choice of a place to go, or *his* special day.

Family Council

One way to get your kids involved in the family process is to have a family council in which everyone is invited to give his or her opinion or viewpoint about a particular matter. This may mean deciding on where or how to spend a vacation; it may be about new adjustments in the family because of Mother taking a job, part or full time; it may be because of a financial setback, how we can all conserve to help make ends meet; or other such problems which involve the whole family. The idea of a family council helps everyone feel an important part of the family, each with his own contribution or ideas. The father, of course, takes charge by leading the discussion, keeping order in the flow of ideas, and then summarizing the conclusions at the end. Each feels a part of the decision.

Allow Them to Learn Some Things the Hard Way

No parent can protect his child from all problems. To do so is a great injustice to the child. He must learn how to handle problems in life as a child before he can handle them in life as an adult. Each child must learn how to take on an ever-increasing amount of responsibility for his own actions and learn how to make intelligent decisions. Some of the best lessons are learned the *hard way,* as the child is allowed to have a few bumps and make some mistakes as a part of growing up. It is helpful after a child has done a few wrong things to learn the value of guilt feelings or disappointments because of his own actions. Experience is still a great teacher and helps him to think ahead on how to make better choices. Some kids do not respond very well to instructions from others and learn no other way but the hard way. For them the parent does best to say what few things he can, but then back off and let the child learn the hard way. The parent can then be available to help as the child puts the pieces together and sees how he can improve for the next time. For example, every parent wishes to prevent his child from wasting his money on junk. However, for a child to learn the value of money and how to control it, he needs a few experiences in which he has wasted it so that he realizes it is gone and he has nothing to show for it. This helps him to learn for himself the importance of conserving his money and not spending foolishly.

Teaching through Example

There is no greater training and counsel than the parent's own example. What you *do* is far more important than what you'll ever *say.* Demonstrating the ways to solve problems by working them out rather than avoiding them gives your child very wise counsel by your own example. Just being able to identify your own problems, and then seeking solutions for them, again helps your child by your example. Forming definite goals for yourself in your own personal growth and maturity, and sharing these goals with the family, gives counsel by example to your child, as he also should develop goals of growth for himself. Showing by your own personal example how to handle problem areas gives invaluable counsel to your own child. Reviewing a few of these with your child helps him to see the steps you've gone through to reach the conclusions, which gives him further guidance as to how to solve his own problems.

Raising kids is basically an art. Part of it is developing the ability to be sensitive to the need of the moment, but also knowing the right time to do such things as: just listen; stretch their thinking process; confront about the wrong kind of behavior; rebuke or discipline; give praise and encourage; touch and hug; intervene; pull back and let them struggle a bit.

The parent who has learned these various skills, and has a deep respect for the individuality of his own child, will usually have a very valuable, open relationship with his or her kids that will enable him to be the counselor and guide that every child needs in facing the hurdles of life.

> Listen, my sons, to a father's instruction; pay attention and gain understanding. I give you sound learning, so do not forsake my teaching. When I was a boy in my father's house, still tender, and an only child of my mother, he taught me and said, "Lay hold of my words with all your heart; keep my commands and you will live. Get wisdom, get understanding; do not forget my words or swerve from them. Do not forsake wisdom, and she will protect you; love her, and she will watch over you" (Proverbs 4:1-6).

> My son, pay attention to what I say; listen closely to my words. Do not let them out of your sight, keep them within your heart; for they are life to those who find them, and health to a man's whole body. Above all else, guard your heart, for it is the wellspring of life (Proverbs 4:20-23).

Workbook Section Chapter Twelve

1. *Our communication as a family*
(circle as applicable):
  a. The communication in our family is (good, bad, so-so).
  b. We (are, are not, are seldom) able to talk over things together or share our thoughts, feelings, and experiences.
  c. My kids (do, do not, seldom) seek my advice or talk about their latest ideas to me as a parent.
  d. I am (happy, unhappy) with the opportunities that I have in helping my kids further develop.

2. *Communication blocks.*
  I may be blocking our communication together by my tendency to (check as applicable):

_____ panic reactions
_____ judgmental attitudes
_____ vindictiveness
_____ overstrictness
_____ overprotectiveness
_____ self-pity
_____ guilt feelings
_____ defeatist attitudes
_____ giving up easily
_____ disinterested attitudes

I can see the need to improve in the areas of: _____

_____
_____
_____
_____

3. *Effectiveness in helping your children.*

Rate yourself as a parent in the following areas using a scale of from one (poor) to ten (good). Try to be honest with yourself.

_____ acceptance as an individual

_____ understanding my child's needs

_____ ability to listen

_____ ability to reason

_____ giving advice, supplying data

_____ demonstrating trust

_____ using a family council

_____ letting children learn some things the hard way

_____ living as an example to be followed

4. *Improvements.*

Some specific things I could do to improve in my weaker areas are:

_____

_____

_____

_____

One of those I would like to work hard on during the next week is: _____

_____

5. *Helping in specific developmental problems.*

A specific problem facing my child right now is:

_____

_____

I can see where I could help him work this out further by:

_____

_____

_____

Thirteen
Letting Go

"I don't understand these kids anymore. Since they've become older, I can't seem to tell them anything. They think they know it all. I just don't know how to get things across to them anymore."

"My kids just want to be out with their own friends all the time. Don't they realize that I gave up many things I wanted to do in order to be with them and take them places? Don't they understand that parents get lonely sometimes and want to do things with them?"

"I've made many sacrifices for my kids. After all the things I've really done for them, you would think they would show some appreciation and consideration; but all they can think of is the things they want to do."

"I can't get over some of the things that my kids try to do. If it weren't for me, they wouldn't be able to make it in this world. They would just fall flat on their faces."

"We enjoy our kids. They visit us and give us opportunity to have fun with the grandchildren. They are busy with their lives and we have our interests also, but we always seem to enjoy our get-togethers."

"I'll be glad when my kids are grown up and gone. Then there will be time for the two of us together. There have been trips that we've wanted to take and places we've wanted to go. Don't misunderstand, we love our kids very much, but we need to get on with our own lives together now."

"I can't wait to get my hands on those grandchildren! I'm going to give them everything their little hearts desire. They're such angels."

All of these are views of parents who have basically raised their kids and are looking at the end of the trail
in parenting responsibility. Different ones adjust in different
ways, some better than others, but each facing a new adjustment to the empty nest syndrome.

A Bewildering Stage

Any parent reaching the stage at which his or her
kids have basically grown up, are in their late teens, or beyond, and facing life for themselves, will do some rethinking
about what all has been happening. It all started with the
early carefree days when just husband and wife were building their nest together with many high ideals and starry-
eyed plans, and with a lot of freedom to come and go when
and where they wished. Those carefree days were abruptly
interrupted when, one by one, children appeared on the
scene. A sudden crimp was put in their freedom to go where
they wanted, and when they wanted. Former interests were
suddenly eclipsed by concerns about diapers, cribs, toys, a
bigger car to accommodate the growing family, a good home,
good schooling, food, clothes, medical expenses, perhaps an
addition on the house, and many new things which required
a great deal of time, patience, and money.

For a few years, you were running after the kids to
keep them from sudden disaster, getting them ready for
school, struggling through their homework, helping them
over the rough spots with their friends, and listening to their
complaints. As time went on, you were running them
everywhere as a somewhat reluctant taxi driver, helping
them through their traumas and newly acquired boy-girl
interests, problems with their peers, struggling through
acne, gawkiness, and feelings of certain ugliness, encouraging them on to days of boredom with school, dates, and any
other problems they could come up with.

As a conscientious parent you've weathered all
these storms and somehow have gotten through. It has taken
all of your money, most of your freedom, and most of your
energy through the years. You may feel that there is little left.

Now what? An even bigger challenge is before
you, that of letting go of the very ones in whom you have

invested your life, energy, and savings. They've gone from total dependency on you to total independence of you, and you're left with the bewildering feeling of no longer being needed, after you've given so much. The children seem to feel that they have graduated from your training school, and there are no new students coming in. You look longingly at empty bedrooms, empty places at the table, recreation rooms that are for once neat and orderly, but also very empty and lonely. Two tired and weather-beaten adults stand alone. The excitement, the hustle and bustle of each day, blend into one quiet day after another. You were needed so much before, but don't feel so needed now.

This may be a time of strain for you. It is very possible that, without realizing it, you made your kids number one in your life instead of each other. The children may have been the main glue to your marriage and the main reason for your struggle together. Once they are gone, the glue may threaten to come apart. Far too many couples have become basically strangers, with little in common except their children through the years. They may have devoted so much time and energy to their kids that they have lost the ability to talk to each other or enjoy each other's company. Some may not be able to make new adjustments to each other again and may choose simply to live together almost as strangers in their own homes, but with their kids in common. Sadly, some marriages will disintegrate in other ways through an affair, separation, or divorce. The empty nest (along with a distance in relationship) is one of the main reasons for divorces after twenty or so years of marriage.

The feeling of loss of control can also be somewhat threatening. Some parents have felt a sense of power and control to be in charge of their children, to map out the strategies for their lives, and to direct their children along the paths of fulfillment of their own dreams for the children. The dreams may include college and careers that the parent himself may not have had the opportunity to realize. It may be pressure toward success that the parent never quite enjoyed for himself; it may be to marry the right person to bring honor or riches to the family; or it may be simply dreams of a very large, impressive church wedding—only to have one son or daughter elope to another state. The parent may have found fulfillment in just being needed, to do things such as help tie shoes, put on clothes, give advice about friends, help with homework, etc. Now the parent no longer feels needed.

The fulfillment of the parent may have come in having complete family activities in which everyone was present and joining in. The parent may have many plans for summers and family outings. Instead, the kids have run off with their group to their own parties with their friends. In such a situation parents can begin to feel a lot of personal rejection and may feel that their children hate them, that somehow they were the wrong kind of parents, when actually the kids have simply developed their own growing independence. A parent can feel crushed when his own teenager seeks advice from another or seems to enjoy visiting the home of another, while the parent sits at home and stares at TV.

It can all be very bewildering. Feelings of rejection, not being loved or lovable as a parent, resentment for all that you have done for them and their apparent lack of appreciation, as well as self-pity become common problem areas for parents at this stage. What is the parent to do? How are parents to handle this whole new situation?

Steps to Take

There are some definite things that each parent needs to do in order to adjust to this new stage in life. Here are some suggestions that will greatly help.

Learn to Let Go

One of the hardest steps that the parent will have to take is to learn to let go of his own children and to let them learn for themselves—even if it means making some mistakes and falling flat occasionally. A parent's immediate instinct is to rush in and protect the children from harm and failure. The role of rescuer seems to be inborn in most parents. It is hard to unlearn that role or restructure it. A parent may find it very difficult to hold back and see his own children suffer as the result of a wrong decision that brings difficulty on himself: to see them go through financial struggles, or to go off with poor attitudes in life. The first impulse is to rush in and help them and to bail them out of their difficulties. However, this is perhaps the worst thing that the parent can do at this point. Do not yield to the temptation. Rather, step back, let them learn for themselves.

The development of personal independence is a vital training stage of the late teens and onward. At this point, the teenager has the basic task of taking hold of responsibilities in life. Any attempt of a well-meaning parent to bail him out will only prolong the dependency, and will bring increasing resentment toward the parent. Prolonging dependency only brings increased fear of the big world that is out there to be faced and conquered, and will bring on a lowering of self-confidence to a teenager, with further drawing back within one's self.

Review again the graphs (that were presented in Chapter One) of the parents' decreasing responsibility and control of a child as time goes on, and the child's increased responsibility for his own self-reliance.

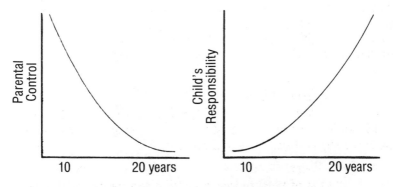

Every counselor has met a distraught parent who has one of his kids at home, eighteen, nineteen, or older, who sits around, does not go out looking for a job, sleeps until noon, and does nothing with his life except go out and party. The parent, at that point, is in a state of panic because he sees a child who should be an adult but is still extremely dependent. The parent has visions of his kid remaining this way for the rest of his life. The problem here is that the child has not been trained to take responsibility. The parent has done it for him, either by intimidation or simply through over-protectiveness and indulgence. He has not trained the child sufficiently to face the outside world. Therefore, at this point he is basically scared, as he doesn't know where or how to start, and will probably need some professional counsel to challenge him to begin, and then to support his uncertain beginning steps.

Some of the basic tasks faced by everyone in the late teens are as follows:

1. Establish one's self in the working world.
2. Find a career.
3. Find life's partner and establish a new home unit.
4. Achieve emotional independence.
5. Achieve competence as a citizen of the community.
6. Sort out one's own set of ethical values as guides to behavior in life.
7. Find one's self spiritually.

Change the Rules

Build a different relationship with your kids. No longer should it be a parent-child relationship, but rather an adult-adult relationship in which there can be give and take with ideas, experiences, and suggestions. Allow your children to learn from their own mistakes, even if it takes them down to the pits. Let them learn for themselves the results of irresponsible decisions, even if it means that they lose out financially. Rejoice with them in the fruit of their own good decisions. There is no teaching in this world that can compare with learning from the school of experience.

As a parent, be prepared to give advice when asked for; otherwise, step back. Learn to hold back the impulse to rush in and solve their problems for them. Learn to bite your tongue, sit on your hands, or whatever you have to do. Simply assure them of your love, whatever decisions they make, and that you will accept them no matter what the consequences.

Another positive thing that you can do is to share memories together. Socialize together on occasions, but try very hard not to be too possessive of them or of their time. Talk about the good times you have had together, and share old experiences. Rejoice with them in their accomplishments and encourage them.

Another thing you can do is share the joy as they become parents. Learn to enjoy your grandchildren. Romp and play with them, but leave the basic discipline of the grandchildren to their own parents. Don't try to take over that area. Neither should you go to the other extreme of showering them with all kinds of gifts. That would only spoil the grandchildren and make it harder for the parents to bring them up right. It would also tend to put feelings of inadequacy on the parents themselves for not being able to supply in the same way.

Revive Your Own Marriage

Undoubtedly your own marriage has suffered a lot of wear and tear by the constant demands and strains of bringing up children. You may be two tired people looking across the table at each other and wondering if you really have anything left of your energy, money, or interests. The wife has the biggest adjustment here, as one of her main tasks in life is now complete. The husband's job continues as ever, which gives him a bit more continuity to his life, but there is no doubt that husbands also struggle with loneliness once the kids are gone.

1. *Plan things together.* This is a time when the husband and wife need to give special attention to further building their own relationship. Each of them should think ahead of things that they can do together and places they can go. They will probably have more money available at this time, and some of this should certainly be used for travel, fulfilling dreams (perhaps a cruise, or just doing a lot of things together that they could not afford the time or money for previously). There are concerts, dinner, special events, a weekend trip, and many other things that can be done. They should look for a certain amount of adventure and new experiences.

2. *Restore romance to your relationship.* Ideally, a couple has tried to maintain some romance in their relation-

ship through the years. But with the pressures of child rear-
ing, making a living, and numerous other responsibilities,
time for romance may have been somewhat less than
adequate. Hopefully, it has not slipped too far and you will
now be able to concentrate more on your own personal life
and restore some of the excitement with each other that was
drowned out by the many demands of your kids. This is a
time for a couple to give more attention to their sex life with
no kids around to interrupt. Take time to do some spontane-
ous and unexpected things on the spur of the moment just
for the fun of it. This won't happen all by itself as you must
take the time to think of things and *do* them, instead of just
collapsing in the chair and staring at the tube.

Find Other Interests
This is the time to develop interests you were unable to explore before. Find some new recreation that you
enjoy, whether it be outdoor things such as camping, boat-
ing, fishing, hunting, or tennis; or interests in some of the
finer arts such as painting, drama, music, photography, etc.
Find something that you enjoy doing and develop it.

Take time to invest in other friends. As you now
have a bit more time available, take time developing deeper
friendships with others of your own basic age level and do
things together.

Invest in hobbies that interest you personally. This
is important, not only now, but also for later years when you
are thinking of retirement and have even more time on your
hands.

The wife may have an interest in working at a job
outside of the home which she may find personally fulfilling. An increasing number are doing this and finding it
stimulating and fulfilling for them, and discovering that the
enrichment of their own personal lives is even of greater
value than the money earned.

Get involved in church and community projects.
Develop interests in other people and other helping organi-
zations besides your own family. This broadens your interest
in others and enriches your own personal life.

Even though you may feel that this is the time to

have a nervous breakdown because you've certainly earned it, take a more positive look, and view this time as yours to build something for yourself to enjoy because you have earned it.

Pray for Your Kids
One of the greatest services you can do for your kids at this time when they have blasted off from your launching pad is to pray for them daily, that they will be committed to God's ways and that he will watch over them and direct their steps. A very clear example of this is found in the life of Job, who prayed daily for his sons, that each of them might be cleansed before God and kept by his power. There is no more quiet but powerful influence upon your now young adult children than a praying parent. This has brought many a wayward child back to the fold and kept many others from straying.

The basic rule in all of this is very simple. Try to *hang onto your kids and they will fight you off.* Then you will suffer grief and hard feelings for many years to come. Or, learn to *let go of your kids and they will be back seeking your fellowship again.* You will enrich their lives, they will enrich yours, and happiness will follow.

The Completed Cycle
The task is now done. You have progressed from the proud parent of a tiny baby to perhaps a bit more humble, but certainly more mature, parent of a young adult. You have worked through the years from when you were totally responsible for this tiny child to the day they have left your control, to be responsible for their own lives. Somehow you may feel that the task doesn't seem quite done; they have not yet learned quite enough. They still seem rather immature and unready; somehow they are just not aware of the many dangers that lurk around the corner of life. You feel that they still desperately need you. How can the task be done when it still seems undone?

I think the answer to this question is found in the Scriptures. In John 17:4, where Jesus was praying in the Garden of Gethsemane shortly before his crucifixion and death for the sins of the world, he prayed to the Father, "I have brought you glory on earth by completing the work you gave me to do." Actually when you look back on three short years of Christ's ministry upon earth, there were many tasks that seemed to be left undone. There were still many towns and villages to which he never preached. His time of ministry was relatively short. He limited his ministry to one small area and basically one language group within the borders of Judea. He wrote down nothing of his teachings. He spent over half of his time just on twelve disciples. Yet, in spite of this, he could say that *he had completed the task* that the Father had given him to do.

In verse six, Jesus continues by saying, "I have revealed you to those whom you gave me out of the world. They were yours; you gave them to me and they have obeyed your word." Even though Jesus was saying that he had completed the task with the twelve disciples and that they had kept the Word of God, yet within one hour's time, every one of them ran away out of fear, and some of them denied that they even knew Christ at all. Jesus knew at that point that they had not learned everything; that they were still very immature and would badly falter at times. However, the basic foundation was laid, and in spite of doubts and difficulties, they would still bounce back and become strong.

Jesus knew clearly that nothing more was needed of his personal attention at that time. He had completed the task that God had given him to do; they were to carry it on from there, and he simply committed them to God for that task.

Can you as a parent say that? Can you say that, "I have completed the task which God has given me to do. I now commit my children to God from here on"? Through the years, you've committed yourself to the task of bringing up these kids, teaching them, training them, correcting them, struggling with them. Now the job is done and they are on their own. Sure, they will falter. Sure, they have immaturities which still need to be worked out, but the basic foundation of their lives has been laid, and the investment that you have made over the years, if done wisely, will certainly pay off rich dividends as time goes on. Even those that seem to get off the track for a time will be getting back on it before long. Commit them now to God, who has simply *loaned* them to you for this important time in their lives, and pray that God will use them in whatever way he chooses.

As you look back, you will realize that all along, *you've been in partnership with God.* God has been alongside of you and directed you through many difficult decisions and struggles. God has lifted you up through times of discouragement and helped you continue. This particular task in your partnership with God is now complete. Rest from your labors and learn to enjoy the fruits of your efforts. Look to God now for a *new area of ministry* in which you may be of help to others in their struggle for growth. You will in this way continue to be in partnership with God, but in a whole new way of ministry.

"For we are God's fellow workers" (1 Cor. 3:9).

"Do your best to present yourself to God as one approved, a workman who does not need to be ashamed and who correctly handles the word of truth" (2 Tim. 2:15).

Workbook Section Chapter Thirteen

1. *"Empty nest" adjustments.*

As a parent with children growing up and leaving home, some of the things facing me are (check those that apply):

_____ loneliness

_____ empty home

_____ bewilderment

_____ not being needed

_____ exhaustion

_____ feeling glad to get rid of them

_____ feeling unsure about the future with my spouse

_____ fear the kids will not make it

_____ feeling fulfilled

_____ feeling glad to see them handle things for themselves

_____ feeling rejected

_____ freedom!

_____ feeling happy to see them grow on their own

Some of the ways I find hard for me to let go are:

_____

_____

I can see that if I do not learn to let go in these areas, it can cause the following problems: _____

_____

_____

Some definite ways I can help my kids develop personal independence are: _____

_____

_____

2. *Strengthening my marriage.*

Some things that I have let get in the way of my marriage are:

_____

_____

_____

Some definite steps I want to take to strengthen my marriage are: _____

_____

_____

_____

Some new activities I would like to be involved in are: _____

_____

_____

_____

3. *Looking back.*

I believe I have been in *partnership with God* to accomplish the following goals in my kids: _____

_____

_____

_____

_____

Bibliography

Brandt, Henry R. and Dowdy, Homer E. *Building a Christian Home.* Wheaton, Ill.: Scripture Press, 1960.

Brown, Francis, Driver, S. R., and Briggs, Charles A. *A Hebrew and English Lexicon.* London: Oxford University Press, 1952.

Christensen, Larry. *The Christian Family.* Minneapolis, Minn.: Bethany Fellowship, 1970.

Dobson, James. *Dare to Discipline.* Wheaton, Ill.: Tyndale House Publishers, 1970.

————. *Hide or Seek.* Old Tappan, N.J.: Fleming H. Revell Co., 1974.

————. *The Strong-Willed Child.* Wheaton, Ill.: Tyndale House Publishers, 1978.

Guernsey, Dennis. "What Kind of Parent Are You?" *Family Life Today,* I No. 2 (Jan. 75), Glendale, Cal.: Gospel Light Publishers.

Ilg, Frances L., and Ames, Louise Bates. *Child Behavior.* New York: Perennial Library, Harper and Row Publishers, 1955.

Kesler, Jay. *Too Big to Spank.* Glendale, Cal.: Regal Books, G/L Publications, 1978.

Kidner, Derek. *The Proverbs, The Tyndale Old Testament Commentaries,* ed. D. J. Wiseman. Downers Grove, Ill.: InterVarsity Press, 1976.

Menninger, Roy. "How to Understand the Perplexing Teen-ager." *Reader's Digest,* Vol. 100, No. 599 (March 1972), Pleasantville, N.Y.: Reader's Digest Association.

Narramore, Bruce. *Help! I'm a Parent*. Grand Rapids, Mich.: Zondervan Publishing House, 1972.

Petersen, J. Allen (ed.). *For Men Only*. Wheaton, Ill.: Tyndale House Publishers, 1973.

————. *The Marriage Affair*. Wheaton, Ill.: Tyndale House Publishers, 1971.

Satir, Virginia. *Conjoint Family Therapy*. Palo Alto, Cal.: a Science and Behavior Books, Inc., 1967.

Steward, Mark A., and Wendkos, Sally Olds. *Raising a Hyperactive Child*. New York: Harper and Row Publishers, 1973.

Swindoll, Charles R. *You and Your Child*. New York: Thomas Nelson Inc., 1977.

Wagner, Maurice E. *The Sensation of Being Somebody: Building an Adequate Self Image*. Grand Rapids, Mich.: Zondervan Publishing House, 1975.

Wright, Norman. *An Answer to Parent-Teen Relationships*. Irvine, Cal.: Harvest House Publishers, 1977.

————. *The Christian Faces . . . Emotions, Marriage and Family Relationships*. Denver: Christian Marriage Enrichment, 1975.